THE HONDA GOLD WING
CLASSIC FOUR-CYLINDER BIKES

PETER RAKESTROW

AMBERLEY

Harry Ward. (Barry W. Benkert, Sr)

1929–2001
I would like to dedicate this book to Harry Ward, who had a vision for a Gold Wing club in Britain. Harry founded what was to become the GWOCGB back in May 1980; I joined in May 1981 and haven't looked back since. If it had not been for Harry Ward's enthusiasm and Soichiro Honda's company my life could have been very different; I would have still bought a Gold Wing because I always wanted one, but who's to say I would have kept buying them, and perhaps I wouldn't have ridden over 280,000 miles on Gold Wings over the years.

First published 2016

Amberley Publishing
The Hill, Stroud,
Gloucestershire, GL5 4EP

www.amberley-books.com

Copyright © Peter Rakestrow, 2016

The right of Peter Rakestrow to be identified as the Author of this work has been asserted in accordance with the Copyrights, Designs and Patents Act 1988.

All rights reserved. No part of this book may be reprinted or reproduced or utilised in any form or by any electronic, mechanical or other means, now known or hereafter invented, including photocopying and recording, or in any information storage or retrieval system, without the permission in writing from the Publishers.

ISBN: 978 1 4456 5717 2 (print)
ISBN: 978 1 4456 5718 9 (ebook)

British Library Cataloguing in Publication Data.
A catalogue record for this book is available from the British Library.

Typeset in 10pt on 13pt Celeste.
Typesetting by Amberley Publishing.
Printed in the UK.

Contents

Introduction	5
1 Concept to Pre-Production	7
2 Production of the Ultimate Sports Motorcycle?	15
3 Evolution to the Ultimate Tourer	37
4 Greater Heights for Honda's Flagship	64
5 The UK Special, the Executive	88
6 Moving to America	92
Acknowledgements	95

To Carroll
All the best
Peter R

Introduction

Back in the 1970s motorcycling was evolving; the British motorcycle industry was on its knees, the Italians were struggling with reliability problems and the Germans were stuck in a rut with old, expensive machines. The Japanese on the other hand had become innovative, developing machines like the Honda CB750, Kawasaki Z900, Suzuki RE5 and, of course, the Honda Gold Wing.

In 1974 journalists looked at the Gold Wing and were asking, 'What is it?' Some loved it, others accepted it and a few said, 'it's a car on two wheels'. Isn't it funny how they didn't say that about the Suzuki RE5 or the Van Veen OCR1000, which in turn were big, heavy machines with very different engines? After all that, what happened to the RE5? It lasted two years and the Van Veen not much longer. The GL1000 Gold Wing should have gone the same way because of the lack of initial sales, but Honda persisted, not only turning it in to the world's most luxurious touring motorcycle, but helping to create a whole new touring after-market industry with it. The other side effect was the emergence of numerous 'owners' groups' around the world, starting in the USA and soon taking off in Europe as well.

So what is Gold Wing? 'It's a luxury touring motorcycle with every amenity fitted to it.' Not quite! 'It's a four-cylinder machine that is now becoming a classic.' This is the problem now with the Gold Wing; some people who own and love the four-cylinder Gold Wings don't like and won't accept the new ones, and some people who buy the latest GL1800 (because they've *always* wanted a Gold Wing) don't even know that the first Gold Wing was a GL1000: 'that's not a Gold Wing,' they say. So I ask again, what is Gold Wing? It's a name Honda gave originally to a motorcycle back in the 1970s that represented their company logo at the time (that was a Gold *Wing*). Mr Honda wanted a motorcycle as a flagship for his company, so from the 'King of Motorcycles' engineering exercise called M1 back in 1972, Honda brought us the GL1000 Gold Wing.

Over the forty years of Gold Wing production, it has appeared with five different engine sizes, from the humble beginnings of a 999cc engine with its four cylinders, through to becoming an 1832cc six-cylinder, although the only thing that remains the same is its name. The Gold Wing has evolved, into what is now a GL1800 luxury tourer. Let's face it – if it wasn't for the GL1000 back in 1974 we might not have the GL1800 Gold Wing today. With around 700,000 Honda Gold Wings sold to date around the world, some journalists must be looking back at the 1970s when the Gold Wing was launched and thinking, 'all of those customers could not have got it wrong!'

This book is concentrating on the era of the four cylinders from 1974 to its end in 1987 with yearly detailed changes; it will also look at the M1 engineering concept in more detail.

Honda's early logo, the Gold Wing. (Peter Rakestrow)

1
Concept to Pre-Production

The great man himself, Soichiro Honda. (Honda Motor Co. Ltd)

1972 M1

Soichiro Honda, a man who had a dream, was very ambitious, a person who would look at things and see them as a challenge and someone who foresaw the needs of others. He was born in 1906 in the tiny village of Komyo, Shizuoka Prefecture, which has now been engulfed by modern-day Hamamatsu. The eldest son of a blacksmith, Soichiro had an eight-year formal education and graduated in 1922; not interested in book learning, he was more interested in the practical approach and at the age of sixteen took an apprenticeship in Tokyo to learn more about the motor car. A number of years later he returned to Hamamatsu to open his own car-repair garage, which became very successful in pre-war Japan. With his newfound wealth he became a bit of a playboy and decided to start racing cars and, after winning a few races, he realised that not only was he a success in business but in racing too. Unfortunately that success was cut short after a crash in 1936 at the All-Japan Speed Rally when a car suddenly pulled across his path at 100 mph. Mr Honda was badly hurt and took eighteen months to recover.

At the age of thirty, Soichiro Honda set up a company to manufacture piston rings, believing that they were a commodity that would always be in demand, but Honda's luck had run out. After employing fifty people, buying a factory and borrowing cash, it turned into a disaster. Undeterred, in November 1937 Honda started a new company called Tokai Seiki Heavy Industries and produced their first acceptable piston ring; Honda was informed that his early efforts lacked silicone in the metal mix. The Tokai Seiki factory was heavily bombed during the war by the Americans, and then was totally destroyed by an earthquake. Later, Honda sold the company to Toyota, who had been one of his customers.

In October 1946, after looking for a business he could put his hand to without any luck, Mr Honda decided to start the Honda Technical Research Institute on a levelled bomb site in Hamamatsu; the institute worked from a tiny 18 × 12 foot wooden hut. Honda bought 500 war surplus petrol engines, which had been used by the military as generators; the genius of Soichiro Honda was his ability to improvise, and he found a way to fix these engines to power pedal cycles. Unable to source any more surplus engines he decided to design his own, building a 50cc two-stroke engine to bolt to a bicycle frame. This officially became known as the 'A-type'. The company had become so successful in only a couple of years that in September 1948 Honda founded the Honda Motor Company Limited.

Over the following twenty-five years Honda's young engineers and designers designed and manufactured motorcycles and cars; it was the brilliance of Takeo Fujisawa, a marketing genius, that pushed Honda forward. By 1969, when the CB750 was launched, Honda was the world's largest motorcycle manufacturer; the CB750's success in part due to a smooth four-stroke single-overhead camshaft (SOHC), four-cylinder air-cooled engine and sleek design features for its day. With the four up-swept exhausts, the engine didn't leak oil and the bike was competitively priced. Kawasaki joined the foray in 1972 with the much heavier and more powerful double-overhead camshaft 903cc Z900 (Z1), with a top speed of 130 mph, 0 to 60 in 4.8 seconds and a standing quarter mile of 12.61 second/105.63 mph. With the Z900, Kawasaki took the four-cylinder engine to even greater heights, with a much faster machine (which is where Kawasaki's heritage lies, speed), and launched a challenge to the CB750. So later that year Soichiro Honda told his engineers that they were to design a motorcycle that would be the 'King of Motorcycles'. This machine was tested, evaluated and then shelved, because it was too long, too fast and not a design that was marketable.

Kawasaki's Z900, the bike that prompted Honda to build the 'King of Motorcycles'. (Peter Rakestrow)

Honda was in the midst of turning the Japanese motorcycling industry upside down again, as they had done in 1969 with the launch of the CB750, but this time it would be a bit different. In late 1972 a young Honda engineer called Shoichiro Irimajiri was to become project leader for one of the most famous motorcycles of all time. Mr Irimajiri and a number of engineers and designers met in a small committee room in Honda's factory at Wako in southern Japan. On this particular day the meeting was to discuss a new project codenamed M1 and called 'King of Motorcycles'. The project was to create a motorcycle that would be the fastest and best grand sports tourer ever built. To achieve this, these young engineers created a machine that was beyond anyone's imagination at the time. The motorcycle in question was to have a wheelbase of 61.8 inches (1,570 mm), a fuel tank capacity of 20 litres and a six-cylinder, water-cooled, horizontally opposed engine with a capacity of 1470cc. The finished bike ran on a 3.25 × 19 inch front tyre and 4.00 × 18 inch rear. The machine weighed in at 484 lbs, being 4 lbs heavier than the CB750, but it felt much lighter because of its low centre of gravity.

The M1 was very much a bike of bits, with parts such as the front end taken from the Honda CB750, with the seat, silencers, gearbox and half of the frame taken from a BMW R75/5 (SWB). Honda cut the frame in half, used the back section and fabricated the front and middle sections. The engine and exhaust down-pipes were made by the Honda engineers, as was the fuel tank, which they made from aluminium and hand-formed. One reason Honda used the BMW was for its shaft final drive, as at the time they didn't have the technology themselves to build one and for new developments it was easier to use other manufacturer's parts that are already proven. The finished M1 also featured saddlebags (made by Wixom), front engine guards and radiator shrouds, which channelled air through the radiator for cooling. The aesthetic look of the M1 was more in keeping with a touring rather than a sports machine.

As with any project, targets or goals must be set, otherwise what would be the aim? The goals set in this case were to build a machine that was capable of more than 130 mph, with peak power of 61 bhp at a high 7,500 rpm; the maximum torque was to be set at 5,500 rpm, which was higher than the machine's cruising speed; and the quarter-mile time goal was 12.40 seconds, which was quicker than the CB750 and Z1. The weight was to be about 463 lbs, divided roughly 40/60 per cent between engine and chassis. The object of the M1's engine was to have the best power to weight and space ratio. The power was to be wide and the torque curve to be flat. All in all the goals set out by the engineers were mainly achieved, except for the weight and power. The finished M1 weighed in 21 lbs heavier and the brake horsepower exceeded the target by 19 bhp (80 bhp at 6,700 rpm). The engine was sand-cast in magnesium and had a bore and stroke of 72 mm × 60 mm. It breathed through a downdraught twin-barrel carburettor, one venturi having a 29 mm bore, the other a 27 mm. These fed into cast inlet-manifolds (a common practice in cars), which were water-cooled. The alternator was positioned at the front of the engine, similar to that of the BMW, and the cooling fan was mechanical, sharing the same shaft as the water pump and driven from the crankshaft. Honda used the BMW R75/5 gearbox, which was a four-speed unit with a dry single-plate clutch bolted to the back of the engine; one problem with this was that it made the engine quite long. On the left-hand cylinder head there was a car-like

Engineering Concept. The M1 was built using a BMW R75/5 (SWB) rear, CB750 front and Wixom panniers. (American Honda Motor Co. Inc.)

distributor, while the coolant reservoir was mounted above the right cylinder head. The radiator was a small unit mounted between the two front frame down-tubes. Its brakes were a single 290 mm disc with leading caliper at the front and a drum at the rear, which was a full-width light alloy unit, with a friction area of 16.55 sq. inches (107 sq. cm).

The M1 took just six weeks to build and was rigorously tested. At one point Mr Honda himself took it for a ride, or so legend has it. Apparently he wasn't keen on the idea of water-cooled motorcycle engines or anything bigger than 750cc, but wanted his young engineers to explore new territory; he apparently said, when he returned, 'It was pretty good, but it looks like a bat'. When the throttle was opened in neutral the bike took on a metallic whine like a Porsche car. So, the bike was pretty good, but the project team decided that they didn't think its design was marketable, and the riding position was not right either. The rider had to stretch to reach the handlebars and controls, which made it very uncomfortable. The Honda engineers knew they had entered new territory and weren't going to give up, and it was decided that the original idea of creating a dual-function motorcycle was asking too much, so the M1 'King of Motorcycles' project was to be split in two. Among other reasons for shelving the M1 bike, but not the project, were that the specifications were incompatible with existing components at the time and the resulting motorcycle would have been too expensive.

Over time the M1 has been changed and mutilated. At one point in the early days it had front crash bars and panniers; then the front end was changed from the CB750 to a GL1100, while the front fender and wire-spoke wheels were from a GL1000. Later the front wheel and fender were replaced with GL1100 units. The M1 is one of the very few engineering exercises (prototypes) to have survived; normally they are crushed, but this motorcycle has been used in further development of the motorcycle Honda were trying to create all those years ago. The M1 now resides at Honda's R&D facility in Japan.

Two pre-production GL1000s. Number 001 in Candy Antares Red and 002 in Candy Blue Green. (Honda Motor Co. Ltd)

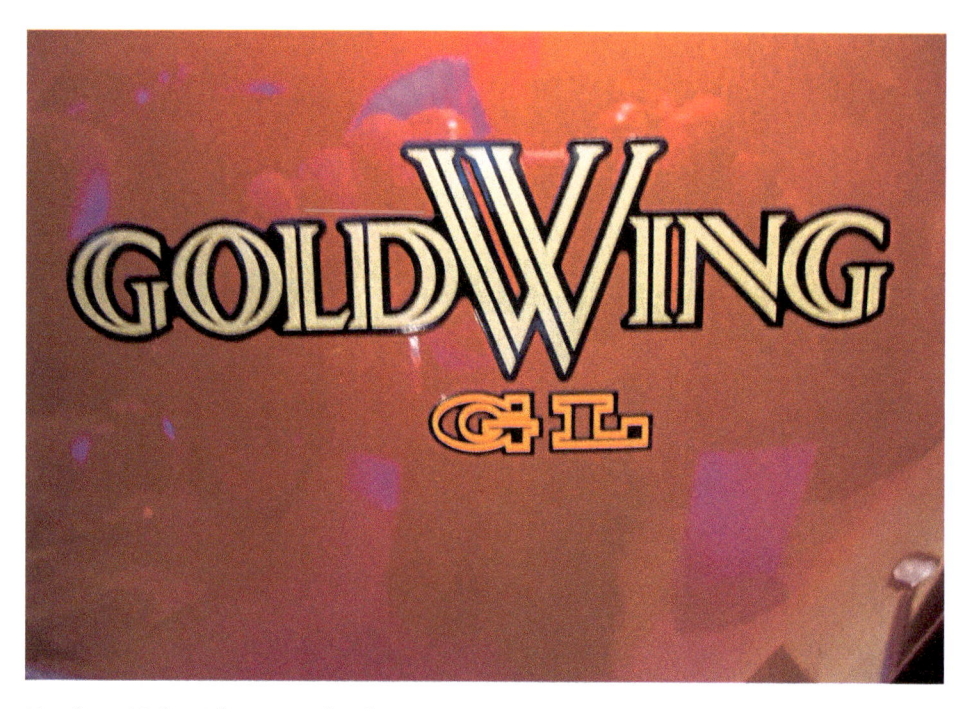

Number 007's side cover decal. It is an exhibit in the Deutsches Zweirad- und NSU-Museum, Neckarsulm, Germany. (Peter Rakestrow)

The pre-production faux tank emblem on number 007. It is an exhibit in the Deutsches Zweirad- und NSU-Museum, Neckarsulm, Germany. (Peter Rakestrow)

1974 GL1000 Pre-Production

Very early in 1973 after the M1 was shelved, Honda engineers started to concentrate more towards the touring aspect of the machine rather than the sports side, although Honda themselves still weren't sure into which category the GL1000 fell. So the project team and engineers set to work on designing a bike with a smaller engine and fewer cylinders. With prototypes being made up and tested throughout 1973 and 1974, most of them being disguised as 750s, Honda got to the point where they had built the final pre-production bikes. Considering Honda had never built a motorcycle with shaft-drive before, it was a very short gestation period from drawing board to a running pre-production bike – about eighteen months. Ten pre-production units were built, although the public only got to see eight of them. Six units went to the USA, one to Germany and the other to France. Five of the six bikes in the States were shown to the press and Honda dealers at American Honda's convention in the luxurious setting of the MGM Grand hotel, Las Vegas, from 19 to 21 September 1974. Two of the units featured small silver nose fairings that Honda had made and were planning on marketing to fit the GL1000 and CB750. The instrumentation on the GL1000 was fitted in the fairing to make it appear part of the bike and not just an add-on. The other three units were placed around the large carpeted conference room of the MGM Grand with other Honda models that were to be marketed for the 1975 season. Three different colours were shown: two units were Candy Antares Red, two units were Candy Blue Green and the last was Sulfur Yellow, which later appeared on the 1976 GL1000 K1.

The pre-production GL1000 with frame number GL1 1000007. This was the one used for the 1974 IFMA Show in Cologne. Some parts are missing; for example, the grab-rail. It is an exhibit in the Deutsches Zweirad- und NSU-Museum, Neckarsulm, Germany. (Peter Rakestrow)

In Germany on 21 September 1974 a Candy Antares Red GL1000 had its world premiere at the IFMA Cologne motorcycle show; this was the first time the public got to see the GL1000 in all its glory. On the same weekend in Le Mans in France, the French public got to see the GL1000 in action at the Bol d'Or race meeting. Honda France had taken delivery of a Candy Blue Green pre-production GL1000 and the plan was to have Jean-Claude Chemarin and Gérard Debrock ride the GL1000 around the race track. Before that, though, Honda France agreed to let a French journalist called F. M. Dumas take the GL1000 for a ride. Dumas was very impressed with the machine Honda had created, saying he was fascinated by its uncanny silence and the tremendous flexibility of the big water-cooled engine. Although he covered little more than 20 miles, he had time to take plenty of photos of the new GL1000 and then sold the story and pictures around the world, his write-up featuring in *Motor Cycle News* 9 October 1974 with the headline, 'The first time test for Tokyo's "formidable" four'. In the meantime, Honda France was getting a rocket from Tokyo. Dumas said, 'My only regret is that Honda [France], who allowed me to ride the fabulous Gold Wing, received a prompt rocket from Tokyo for letting me enjoy a world scoop.'

2

Production of the Ultimate Sports Motorcycle?

1975 GL1000K0 (Project 371)

Once the shows had come and gone the European press didn't know quite how to take the GL1000; the Americans, however, greeted it with more warmth. Honda's big plan was to sell the GL1000 Gold Wing to the American market anyway, as the Americans seem to like much bigger things. The only comparable motorcycles available to American buyers were expensive BMWs and their home-grown Harley-Davidson Electro-Glides, which were so unreliable.

Before Honda started mass production of the GL1000, most of the parts on the pre-production bikes were redesigned, including the cylinder heads, faux tank unit, water-pump housing, fuel tank, switchgear, front fender and even the fork-legs, either for ease of production or for cost-saving reasons. Some nice features that were taken away from the production models were the latches for opening the faux tank side panels, the top faux tank emblem which read 'Gold Wing GL1000 water cooled Honda' and also the 'Gold Wing' printed on the rear of the seat. One other thing that was way ahead of its time was the self-cancelling turn signals; the system was complicated and bulky, and so was also removed.

Production started in December 1974 with the GL1000K0 models (export only); built at the Saitama factory (Sayama Plant), which had a 162,100 sq. metre floor area and employed around 3,900 people, the unique thing about this particular factory at the time was that it also produced Honda automobiles, the Accord and the Civic 1500.

Other revolutionary motorcycles such as the CB750K0, with its sandcast, air-cooled four-cylinder, single overhead camshaft engine, became instant success stories, but with the GL1000, with its horizontally opposed four-cylinder engine, what was it? This was a motorcycle, or was it? Motorcycles were getting bigger from all corners of the globe, which was very obvious at the 1974 Cologne motorcycle show with the likes of Van-Veen, a Dutch company that produced a very expensive rotary-engined machine, the OCR1000. This also applied to Suzuki at the Tokyo motorcycle show the year before, where they launched the 500cc RE5, a big motorcycle for its engine size, and Moto-Guzzi with its V1000 Convert. So what of the GL1000? The French journalist F. M. Dumas had ridden the bike earlier and said

1975 Candy Blue Green GL1000 K0. (American Honda Motor Co. Inc.)

The opened faux tank with tool tray, kick-starter lever and coolant reservoir. (Peter Rakestrow)

The GL1000's forty-spoke wire wheel with twin 275mm discs. (Peter Rakestrow)

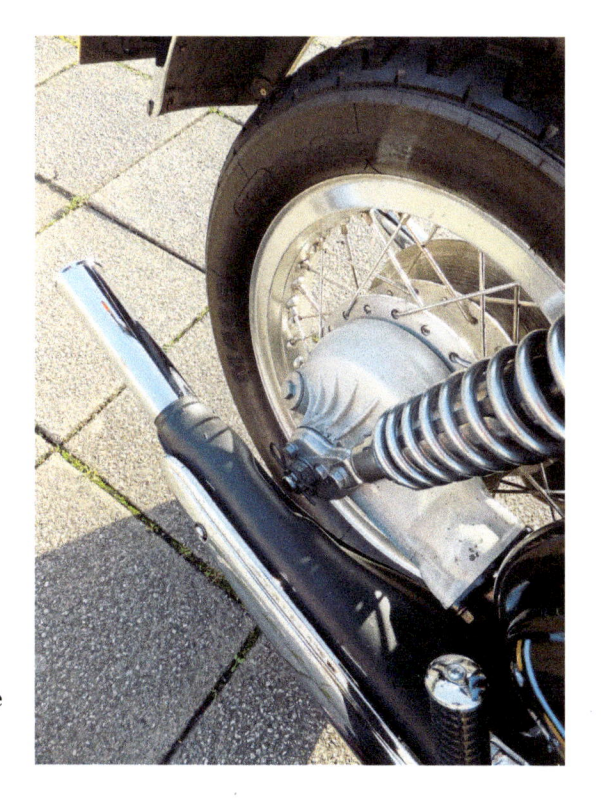

The GL1000's differential along with the rust-prone exhaust that everybody now wants! (Peter Rakestrow)

17

The removable kick-starter lever inserted into the back of the engine. (Peter Rakestrow)

it was fabulous, but it wasn't until other journalists, especially British ones, rode it that people realised the Gold Wing wasn't as bad as they had first feared. Some just didn't want to accept it (a car engine in a motorcycle frame!), and even Honda themselves weren't sure into which category the Gold Wing fitted. The bike's looks belied its weight, with its low centre of gravity coming from the opposed configuration of its four cylinders and the gearbox below those cylinders, which meant most of the engine weight was very low – the whole engine weighed 234 lbs dry (106 kg), which was 40 per cent of the bike's total weight of 584 lbs dry (265 kg). The fuel tank was located under the seat, which was very unconventional at the time. Again this was done just to keep the bike's mass low. The engine was 999cc with a bore and stroke 72.0 × 61.4 mm and breathed through 4 × 32 mm Constant Velocity-type carburettors (similar to the ones Honda had used in their S800 sports car), which made the bike smooth, quiet and well balanced. Torque reaction was non-existent, and this was achieved by a clever idea from the engineers of turning the clutch counter-clockwise to the cylinders and the alternator clockwise. This counter balanced the engine when the throttle was opened sharply. Water-cooling made the engine quiet but, to stop the chatter of timing chains, the engineers decided to use inverted-toothed rubber belts. The GL1000 has its cylinders cast into the main crankcases, so there are three parts to one side of the engine: the crankcase, cylinder head and rocker cover. This engine sat in one of the largest frames Honda had ever built for a motorcycle; the double cradle tubular steel frame with 32 mm down-tubes, compared to the CB750's 29 mm, was huge by motorcycling standards.

The Gold Wing GL1000's 4.2 imperial gallon (19 litres) under-seat fuel tank. (Peter Rakestrow)

With Honda, new territory had certainly been broken; the GL1000 was a totally new concept to motorcycling with many new technologies and firsts. It was the first Honda motorcycle with a thermostatically controlled water-cooled engine, as well as the first to be shaft-driven and have three hydraulic stainless steel disc brakes, two single-piston calipers (275 mm) at the front and one twin-piston caliper (295 mm) at the rear. The wheels were forty-spoke wire with aluminium DID rims, the rear being just 17 inch with a newly developed tyre size (4.50-17) to cope with the bike's load capacity – the largest Honda had ever fitted to a motorcycle. There was a faux tank, which housed the electrics on the left-hand side, with its reserve lighting system (US and Canadian markets only), and the cooling reservoir tank and emergency kick-starter lever on the right. The centre section housed the tool-tray/storage compartment. The faux tank could only be opened with the ignition key; after opening the top flap and removing the tool/luggage tray it then revealed two turn-screws that unscrewed and let the tank sides fold down. The fuel gauge in the centre section of the faux tank was another first for a Honda motorcycle, although it did not prove to be very accurate. The GL1000's gearbox is complex with numerous moving parts; this caused some complaints from customers about it being too clunky. It had five gears operated through a wet multi-plate clutch, which used some clutch plates from a CB450, while the clutch springs were first used on a CB72 Hawk 250.

The Gold Wing GL1000's dimensions were in keeping and well in proportion, with a long wheelbase of 1,545 mm (60.9 inch), which was 90 mm (3.6 inch) longer than the CB750K,

The first GL1000 American brochure, featuring a pre-production unit, surrounded by each American GL1000 sales brochure in date order, starting from the left. (Peter Rakestrow)

The author's cut-away GL1000 engine that he and his brother built. Model year 1976 K1, seen here are the timing belts and valve gear. (Peter Rakestrow)

Another view, showing the spring from the output shaft, the fuel pump and exhaust downpipes. (Peter Rakestrow)

and a seat height just slightly higher than the CB750's of 810 mm (31.9 inch). The fuel tank capacity was 4.2 imperial gallons (19 litres).

The GL1000K0 Gold Wing was released to American dealers in March 1975, with two colour options available: Candy Antares Red and Candy Blue Green. These are the same two colours that appeared on the pre-production units; the only difference was that the lower Gold stripe was now straight and the side cover decal read 'GL1000'.

The US publication *Cycle*, in its first full test on the GL1000 Gold Wing in the April 1975 issue, featured Phil Schilling riding one of the pre-production units on the front cover with more colour pictures of the bike inside. The test itself was conducted using a production GL1000 as well. *Cycle* performed a standing start quarter-mile test just to see how quick this thing was and, after four runs, the bike returned a best of 13 seconds at 102.38 mph, but the clutch was knackered, so the bike was returned to Honda for a new clutch and a tune-up, returned back to *Cycle* and put through its paces again. This time it returned a standing quarter mile of 12.92 seconds at 104.52 mph. This was slightly slower than the Kawasaki Z1, making the Gold Wing GL1000 the second fastest production motorcycle at the time, although the GL1000 was 74 lbs heavier. Despite this, the American buying public was not convinced and sales for the first model were way down from the expected target of around 60,000 units, which had been very ambitious from Honda. In reality about 5,000 GL1000K0's were sold worldwide.

1976 GL1000K1

Honda worked very hard in the early months of 1975 to market the GL1000, with Honda (UK) bringing onto British soil three US-specification Gold Wings for press and public evaluation. In January 1975 Honda (UK) held a dealer seminar known as 'Honda Expo 75' where they displayed the GL1000K0. Prior to this, on 28/29 October 1974, Honda (UK) displayed the Cologne pre-production unit at the 'Two Wheeler Dealer' trade show, which was held at the London Hilton Hotel in Park Lane. In May/June 1975 Honda (UK) took all three US GL1000s to the Isle of Man for TT week, where the press were allowed to ride them around the circuit, but under strict instructions not to rev the bikes over 5,000 rpm. As part of a 'tribute to Mike Hailwood' Honda fitted a plaque to the headlamp of one GL1000 and gave Mike the opportunity to ride the bike around the circuit but, unfortunately, due to a limp from a car racing accident, he was unable to ride the huge Gold Wing, though he was happy to sit on the back with Geoff Duke in control.

In August 1975, at the Earls Court Motorcycle Show, Honda displayed the first UK specification GL1000 Gold Wing to the public during the same week the bike had also been released to dealers. The price set was a reasonable £1,600, though earlier expectations had been around £1,800. The interesting thing was that these were GL1000K1s (1976 models). The first noticeable difference to the K0 model was the lower pinstripe on the faux tank; there were now two stripes, one being gold, the other orange. The instruments had also been altered from having dark-green faces to being a much lighter green. Models for different markets have always differed and the UK-specification Gold Wing was no exception. The GL1000K1 was fitted with lower handlebars (as we ride much faster than the Americans), a longer rear mudguard and a smaller rear light unit with a black painted bracket, as opposed to the American model's chrome-plated one. For the 1976 model three colour options were offered, which were the same as the pre-production units in 1974. Candy Antares Red and Candy Blue Green were sold in the UK, while the Americans had a choice of Candy Antares Red and Sulfur Yellow.

A promotional 1,000-piece jigsaw puzzle of the GL1000 K0, sold in Honda dealerships in the 1970s. (Peter Rakestrow)

1976 GL1000 K1, a nice UK-specification example. Note the flat handlebars and small rear light. (Peter Rakestrow)

Throughout 1976 the GL1000K1 was modified and problems sorted out. One problem was the lack of a nipple to grease the splines on the final drive pinion shaft. This was fitted so that the owner or dealer, while maintaining the bike, didn't have to remove the rear wheel and differential every 6,000 miles to grease them. One other convenient change was to the oil sight glass, which was fitted with a wiper. This was done so the owner could clean the glass to check the oil level; the window itself is not very big and awkward to see. The gear pedal was altered, with the rubber made wider and flatter instead of small and round. On top of the carburettors there is a chrome bracket, which has a clip to hold the HT leads. This was extended to cover the throttle linkage, and the linkage itself was also altered from substantial solid bars to flatter pressed steel ones. The switch gear on the GL1000 up to the K2 was made of cast aluminium and on the GL1000K0 and early GL1000K1s the clutch lever bracket was cast into the switchgear. Honda found that, with the heavy clutch on the GL1000, this could possibly crack, so the clutch lever bracket was made separate to the switchgear, making the clutch lever longer, which in turn made the clutch feel lighter due to the extra leverage.

Honda (UK)'s second batch of K1s came in with even more changes, as the headstock bearings were changed from ball bearing to a tapered-roller type. The battery box was totally redesigned, with the early GL1000s having just a large rubber band to hold the battery in the steel box. Honda thought this wasn't good enough and so altered it to a bar hinged from the bottom of the box with a rubber strap fixed on the top. The faux tank got a look at as well; the large turn-screws that hold the sides of the tank closed had a tendency of falling out when the sides were opened, so Honda fitted screw-on washers to them so that they stayed in position – a simple but welcome addition. The air-filter box had a bit of treatment too; the lid was fixed with one wing-nut, and this was altered so that the lid had two nuts holding it on, making a greater seal. Little subtle changes make all the difference: the cam-belt covers were redesigned by casting a drain vent on the bottom edge so that condensation would dry out from them, and the rocker box covers and emblems (now black) were also modified. The emblems were now fixed with two screws instead of being a push fit. The problem with the push-fit system was that the engine got hot and the emblem had a tendency to fall off.

As the GL1000 was now available in more countries, momentum was growing, but it wasn't until the release of the GL1000 LTD to American customers in May 1976 that Gold Wing sales started to rise rapidly. The marketing side of Honda got in on the act too and produced a 1,000-piece jigsaw puzzle of the K0, a snip at only £3 plus VAT (at a rate of 8 per cent).

1976 GL1000K1 LTD

This was the second model year of the GL1000 and Honda produced a limited edition Gold Wing. The 1976 GL1000K1 LTD was to commemorate the bicentennial anniversary of America, with American Honda Motor Co. Inc. importing 2,000 of these special 'GLs' from Japan. On 26 May 1976 a letter and 'dealer only' single-page brochure were sent out by Mr S. Tanaka, National Sales Director for the Motorcycle Division. The letter told the dealers about twelve important features of the GL1000 LTD. Described as 'pieces of art', these bikes were crafted using methods that would usually only be employed by custom bike builders, with special attention to detail, an array of chrome and deep paintwork with even more pinstriping.

Two things stand out on this Gold Wing. First is the deep Candy LTD Maroon paint work with its gold pinstriping; Honda added more striping to the sides of the faux tank, and the top of the faux tank also had a stripe around its edge. The side covers now had a stripe that followed the curve of the cover and went around the beautiful LTD emblem and Gold Wing decal. The second is the wheels with their forty gold-anodised spokes and aluminium rims. For the LTD the seat was re-contoured and sported a new ribbed quilt-pattern, the Honda printed in gold on the rear was deeper, and a chrome trim was added from one side around the back to the other side. The engine had different treatment as well; the engine cases were painted in a specially formulated metallic-silver paint and all the bolts were chrome-plated. The engine breather filter had the top chromed and the top engine hanger brackets were chromed instead of black (as on the K0 and K1). Other items to have the chrome treatment were the rear exhaust brackets, side stand, differential oil filler cap, radiator side shrouds and the rear foot-pegs, which now featured chrome ends that screwed on. The engine heat shield attached to the alternator cover on the left of the bike, which is painted silver on the K0 & K1, was also chrome-plated.

A European-specification 1976 GL1000 K1 LTD, complete with leather LTD panniers. (Peter Rakestrow)

Other items changed on the LTD were the instruments. Instead of the green faces as on the standard K1 model, they were black. The handlebars were higher for a more 'sit-up and beg' type riding position. The emblem on the top of the faux tank of the standard 'GL', which is black with a silver/chrome edge, made of a plastic card material and reads 'GL1000 Honda', became a metal emblem that was black with a gold edge, with the writing embossed 'Gold Wing GL1000'. The Honda emblems on the sides of the faux tank were solid gold-on-black, longer, and handed left and right, as they now curved to the front of the faux tank. The side-cover emblems have a black base with the two eagles kissing the red LTD shield. The outline of the eagles is in gold but the wings, body and tail colour is Candy LTD Maroon, with the socks and head in white. It's this sort of detail that makes this bike special.

The GL1000K1 Limited Edition is now one for the collectors. Thinking of buying one? Make sure it's complete with owner's manual, key fob and tool kit. The owner's manual is covered in a leather-type material and of a gold-brown colour, with the LTD emblem printed in gold. The pages are a nice glossy paper that has a gold edge to it – again, Honda's attention to detail. For a bike built in the mid-1970s it has to have the best, most luxurious tool kit ever offered on a motorcycle; twenty-eight pieces, fully chrome-plated, wrapped in a gold-brown leather case. It comprised a socket set, hexagonal wrenches, a file, multi-feeler gauge set and even a tyre-pressure gauge. This was on top of all the bits in the standard K1's tool kit. The key fob is made of darker-brown leather and is designed to hold one ignition key. The key itself is attached to a leather strap, which, when not in use, retracts into the key fob and then clips to the outside by way of a push stud. This also has the LTD emblem embossed on it.

A display of the GL1000 K1 LTD's leather key fob, side-cover emblem and tank-top emblem, along with three leather-bound owner's manuals for the American, European and Canadian models. (Peter Rakestrow)

Although about 3,400 in total were built and other countries around the world were fortunate to have the GL1000K1 LTD officially imported by Honda, unfortunately the UK did not; so Honda (UK) invited Rickman Brothers to build their own Limited Edition Gold Wing in the form of the GL1000K1 Executive (see chapter five), to be marketed in early 1977.

1977 GL1000K2

After the success of the LTD, Honda kept improving the Gold Wing even more and tried to keep the sales momentum going. Under project leader Masaru Shirakura, changes to the GL1000K2 were mainly cosmetic (with parts continuing on from the LTD), although they did want to make the Gold Wing even quieter; to achieve this Honda increased the thickness of the K2 engine cases to lessen engine chatter. The engine hangers and heat shield on the alternator were now chrome-plated, as on the LTD. One other thing they wanted to achieve was to make the bike more comfortable, so they made the handlebars 2.6 inch (67 mm) higher than the K1's. The seat was now stepped and similar to the LTD's, just a different part number. All this was great for the American and Canadian buyers, but the UK market still had the flat handlebars and ironing board seat from the previous model. Although the rear seat chrome trim was included, it didn't do much for its comfort! The handlebar grips were now made of neoprene instead of the plastic waffle-type ones used on the K0/K1, and they also had chrome end inserts.

Other changes included a special treatment to the inside of the petrol tank to stop rust. The faux tank had more pinstriping than the K1 and instead of the lower tank stripes being straight they now followed the line up the front of the panel; the side covers, like the LTD's, got the stripe treatment too. The faux tank panels got new 'Honda' emblems similar to the LTD's, again handed left and right. The other distinguishing feature on the K2 was the new chrome down-pipe covers. The problem with the down-pipes was with the heat and being vulnerable to water and road grime; they would tend to rust and look unsightly. One feature on the UK model of the K2, which made life a bit easier when fitting panniers, was that Honda moved the rear indicators from under the seat, where they were fitted to the grab-rail, relocating them next to the larger rear light unit.

Unfortunately all of these improvements came at a cost, with the UK price increasing by a whopping 25 per cent to £1,995. Three colours for the K2 were offered, two new (Black and Candy Sirus Blue), with Candy Antares Red continuing.

The changes to the Gold Wing for 1977 were recognised by the motorcycle press industry with *Cycle World* (an American publication) in its second annual 'The Ten Best Bikes' feature awarding it the title of 'Best Touring Bike'. Honda themselves were determined that the Gold Wing would be a success, with its sales picking up after the GL1000 LTD was marketed. Plans were afoot to build a factory in the USA, the chosen location being Marysville, Ohio.

Other manufacturers were getting in on the emergence of this market Honda was building; all the other three big Japanese manufacturers were starting to offer multi-cylinder, shaft-drive motorcycles, but Honda had the edge. In its short history the Gold Wing had already attracted a following with rider groups forming in the USA (Gold Wing Road Riders Association) and, the following year, in some European countries, including The Netherlands, Germany and Switzerland.

The author's original Gold Wing, a 1977 GL1000 K2 purchased in 1980 that has covered over 140,000 miles. (Peter Rakestrow)

1978 GL1000K3 (Project 431)

The GL1000 had now entered its fourth year of production with a complete redesign from the ground up; by this time Honda had decided that its Gold Wing was a tourer and not necessarily a performance bike. The people who were buying the Gold Wing were kitting them out with fairings and saddlebags and loads of chrome accessories; a whole aftermarket industry had suddenly sprung-up. Honda realised that they had a band of unpaid test riders evaluating the product; taking this on board they incorporated the feedback into the new model's design. For the '78 model year Honda engineers set-to to give the Gold Wing more torque than power by changing the valve timing and reducing the carburettor size from 32 mm to 31 mm. The brake horsepower (bhp) was reduced from 80 to 78 bhp and the maximum torque of 60 ft lb was achieved at 950 rpm lower than the previous models. This in turn reduced the top speed, but the customers weren't interested in how fast these bikes went; they were more interested in overtaking speed and acceleration when cruising, comfort, range and how much luggage they could carry.

To accommodate these factors the frame was redesigned and strengthened and the engine had some modifications, with a primary chain (Hy-Vo) tensioner fitted, as some early GL1000s did seem to rattle a bit if the carbs were out of synchronisation. The kick-start mechanism was removed, which wasn't a bad thing as it rarely got used and had a tendency to seize up. The faux tank was redesigned, giving a more bulbous look. The tank top now opened from front to back and was covered in an imitation leatherette, and the K3 also featured a new GL1000 eagle-like emblem. The Honda emblems were changed again,

1978 GL1000K3 in exceptional condition. Note the reshaped faux tank and smaller side-covers. The colour is Candy Limited Maroon. (Peter Rakestrow)

The GL1000 clutch in its steel basket, which rotates counter-clockwise to the engine. (Peter Rakestrow)

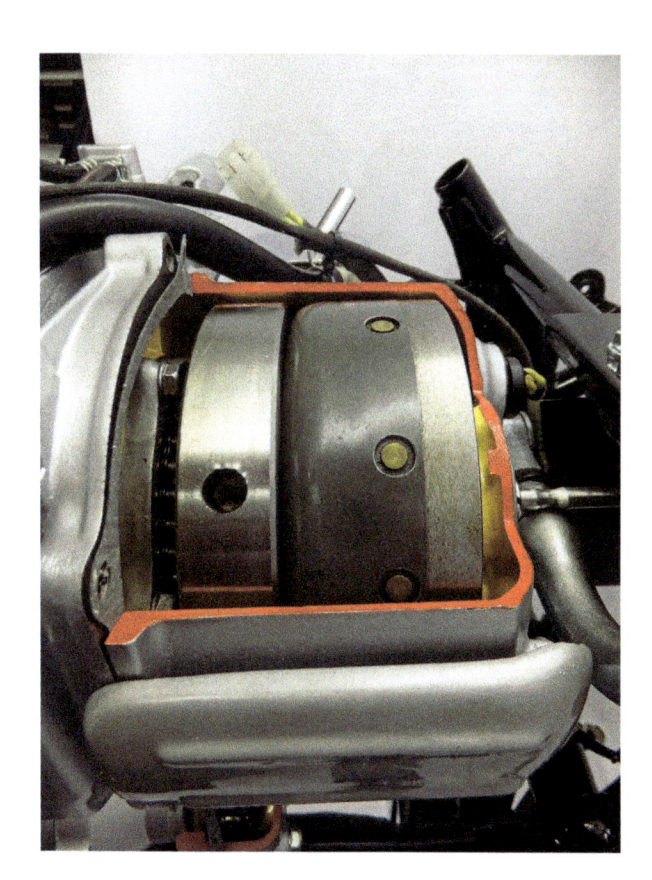

The 300 watt alternator that turns the opposite way to the clutch, alleviating torque-reaction. (Peter Rakestrow)

The five-speed gearbox that sits under the crankshaft. Also the double-walled cut-away downpipe. (Peter Rakestrow)

The GL1000 carburettors, four 32 mm CV type, similar to the ones used on Honda's S800 sports car. (Peter Rakestrow)

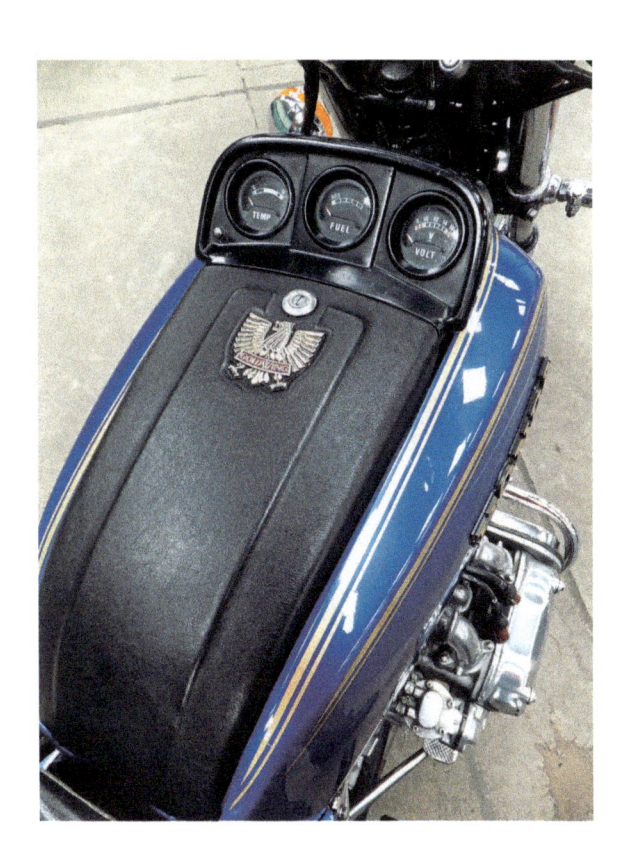

The instruments on the 1978 K3 and 1979 Z. The K3's instrument needles are red. Note the leatherette top shelter cover with emblem. (Peter Rakestrow)

to shorter, straighter ones. Three instruments now resided on the faux tank: a fuel gauge, temperature gauge and new volt meter. The speedometer and tachometer were redesigned and all the instruments featured red needles. The side covers were made much smaller and now featured a 'Gold Wing GL1000' emblem as opposed to decals. The front suspension had been improved to stop some of the static friction and the brake caliper fixing points were altered. The rear shock absorbers that were now FVQ type had two-stage dampening, but didn't make that much improvement to the ride. The swingarm now featured an extension on the left side with a hole, which was to tie the arm up and make things easier when having to change the rear tyre.

Honda's new invention, the ComStar wheel, was used on the GL1000 for the first time. Both wheels had aluminium rims with aluminium spokes but, soon after the bike's release in the States, Honda announced a recall, saying, 'When the front brake is applied under certain combinations of speed and special road surface conditions, a resonance may occur causing the spoke blade near the rim to crack and the wheel could collapse.' These wheels were replaced with units that had steel spokes; the rear wheel wasn't affected. The front discs and calipers used from the CB750F2 were a lighter, five-spoke combination. One big noticeable change was the exhaust system; on earlier models customers complained that the bike was a bit too quiet and also that the system was prone to rusting, so the K3 model had an all-new system that was chrome-plated, the balance box was replaced with a single pipe and the silencers were now in two pieces – an audible difference was a throatier sound. The K3's seat had been redesigned with a two-layer foam construction; over the years Honda did have a problem with being able to make a comfortable seat. The new seat had a different quilted pattern and was squarer at the back. Up front illumination improved with a headlamp using a H4 halogen lamp encased in a lighter black plastic headlamp shell. Like the UK's K2 model, Honda relocated the rear indicators to beside the tail light. The switchgear was totally new and made from plastic, not cast aluminium as on the previous models; the cables now ran externally (this made the changing of the handlebars easier); also Honda fitted a 5 amp accessory terminal in the left side of the faux tank so owners could power C.B. and AM/FM radios. It was also decided to do away with the reserve lighting system from the earlier GL1000s. Dual (Hi-Lo) horns were a welcome addition as the previous single unit was a bit pathetic. Gone was the plastic bag for the tool kit; the K3s tools were wrapped in a cloth tool roll. Despite the use of lighter plastics on some of the parts, the bike's weight increased to 601 lbs (273 kg) dry.

Three colours were offered for this year: Candy Grandeur Blue Special, Candy Limited Maroon and black. All had double gold pinstriping with closed ends. Honda (UK) didn't officially import this model as they had plenty of K2's left to sell.

Early in 1978 Honda announced a recall for a brake problem on GL1000s after complaints from customers. The US Department of Transport carried out an investigation on reports of poor wet-weather braking. Initially they thought the problem was with the front brakes, but found in fact it was the rear brake, and Honda issued a safety recall covering all previously sold Gold Wings, having redesigned the rear brake pads.

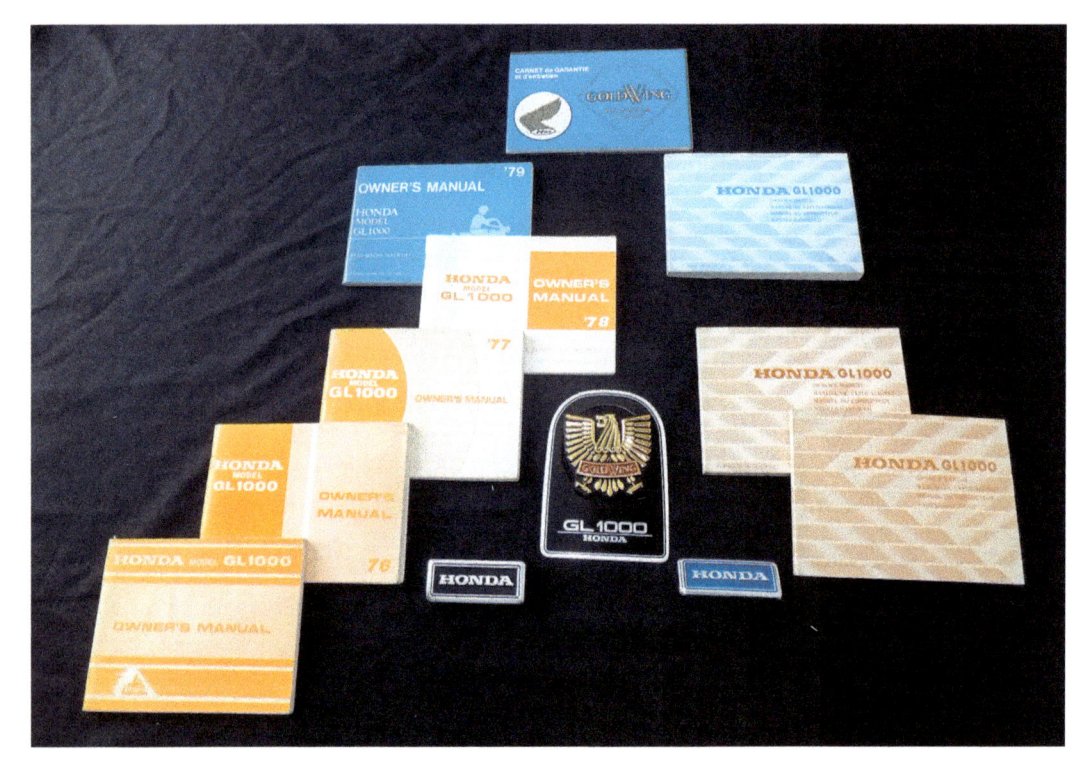

GL1000 owner's manuals and emblems. American manuals on the left in date order and UK manuals on the right with a French service book at the top. (Peter Rakestrow)

1979 GL1000Z

1979 is the most confused year in the Gold Wing's history; this year's model has been known as a K3, but also known as a KZ in Britain or a K4. Actually it is none of these; it is simply 'Z'. I know Honda (UK) refer to it as a 'KZ' but it is just plain 'Z'. So why is the designation a 'Z' and not a 'K4'? In 1979 Honda along with other manufacturers decided to use what is known as the Alpha System to designate model years and it started with 'Z' (1980 = A) and ended in model year 2000 with a 'Y'. Letters such as I, O, Q and U were not used.

There is also confusion about the GL1000Z and the K3. When looking at the two bikes quickly they seem the same, but they are actually quite different. Look at the front discs on the 'Z', they have five twin spokes and were from the CBX, along with the calipers, replacing last year's CB750F2 units. The ComStar wheels have larger steel spokes; this made them much stronger than the previous year's, which had been problematic. The instruments are different, now with white needles replacing the red ones on the K3. The colours Honda used in 1979 were the same three colours as the previous year; the striping was different, still gold in colour, but the ends at the top of the double stripe were now open. The brake and clutch levers were anodised black and the handlebars were reduced by 30 mm in height as customers complained they were just too high. The US and Canadian specification

The smaller side cover of the GL1000K3/Z, with emblem as opposed to the earlier decals. (Peter Rakestrow)

The author's GL1000K2, 'blinged-up' in 1992 before it was returned to a naked GL1000. (Peter Rakestrow)

'79 models featured a larger CBX-style rear light unit with rectangular indicators and a rectangular front brake master cylinder, while the UK buying public still got the same units that were fitted to the K2 model. For the UK market only one colour was offered, black, and yet again the price increased, this time to £2,295.

By this time Honda's accessories division, Hondaline, were making more optional extras for the Gold Wing by way of front engine bars, luggage racks, saddlebags and top case. These detached by key, had handles and were more like suitcases, as depicted on the front cover of the American 1979 sales brochure.

On 10 September 1979 Honda America Manufacturing (HAM) started production in the new Marysville Motorcycle Plant (MMP); the plant was built to produce the Gold Wing (as American Honda now sold about 80 per cent of Gold Wing production). The first machines to be built in the plant were the CR250R Elsinore, as these were deemed simple machines to build for the new employees, who were ex-farm hands with no previous experience in building motorcycles (see chapter six).

Specifications

GL1000 1975–1979
Dimensions
Overall length	K0/K1/K2	2,305 mm (90.8 inches) [2,330 mm (91.7 inches)] {2,340 mm (92.1 inches)}
	K2/Z	[2,350 mm]
	K3/Z	2,320 mm (91.3 inches)
Overall width	K0/K1	875 mm (34.4 inches) [760 mm (29.9 inches)] {760 mm (29.9 inches)}
	LTD/K2/K3/Z	920 mm (36.2 inches) [765 mm (30.1 inches)] {765 mm (30.1 inches)}
Overall height	K0/K1	1,225 mm (48.2 inches) [1,150 mm (45.3 inches)] {1,150 mm (45.3 inches)}
	LTD/K2/K3	1,265 mm (49.8 inches)
	Z	1,235 mm (48.6 inches)
Wheel base		1,545 mm (60.9 inches)
Ground Clearance		140 mm (5.5 inches)

Weight
Dry weight	K0/K1	265 kg (584 lbs)
	K2	270 kg (595 lbs)
	K3/Z	273 kg (601 lbs)
	Z (US spec)	274 kg (604 lbs)

Engine
Bore and stroke	72.0 × 61.4 mm (2.834 × 2.417 inches)
Compression ratio	9.2:1
Displacement	999cc (61.0 cu-in.)
Carburettors	K0 - K2 4 × 32 mm CV Keihin
	K3 - Z 4 × 31 mm CV Keihin
Power output	K0 - K2 80 bhp @ 7,000 rpm
	K3 - Z 78 bhp @ 7,000 rpm

Power transmission
Primary reduction		1.708
Secondary reduction		0.825
Gear Ratio	1st	2.500
	2nd	1.708
	3rd	1.333
	4th	1.097
	5th	0.939
Final reduction		3.400

Chassis and suspension
Castor   62 degrees
Trail   120 mm (4.7 inches)
Tyre size   Front   3.50 H 19 (4PR)
                  Rear   4.50 H 17 A (4PR)

Electrical
Battery   12v–20AH
Generator output   300 watt @ 5,000 rpm A.C. Three phase

Note: [ ] UK type.
         { } European type.

3
Evolution to the Ultimate Tourer

1980 GL1100A and GL1100IA Interstate (Project 463)

In the States, the touring sector of motorcycling was really starting to take off, with all the other three big Japanese manufacturers offering bikes with shaft-final-drive, including Yamaha with their XS1100, Suzuki's GS850, both air-cooled in-line fours, and Kawasaki with its behemoth KZ1300, a heavyweight water-cooled six-cylinder machine. This left the Gold Wing again out of date and in need of more of everything. Honda responded to the call and released an all-new Gold Wing in the form of the GL1100, although the engine's architecture was the same, just bored-out to 75.0 × 61.4 mm (2.95 × 2.42 inch), which gave the bike 1085cc up from 999cc. The rest of the GL1100's internals were strengthened, the crankshaft had larger diameter journals, the primary chain (Hy-Vo) increased in width by a quarter inch (6 mm) and the valve lift and timing were revised. All of this was done to cope with the increase in power and torque, with the claimed power output increasing from the K3/Z's 78 bhp to 81 bhp.

Yamaha's XS1100, with an air-cooled four-cylinder engine and shaft-drive. (Peter Rakestrow)

Kawasaki's Z1300 and the Yamaha XS1100 were both stiff competition for the Gold Wing. (Peter Rakestrow)

The aesthetics of the engine itself were different with new shaped rocker-box covers. These had 'GL' and '1100' cast into them along with 'Made in Japan'. The back engine casing was longer; this was to accommodate the new electronic ignition system, which was state of the art vacuum advanced (no more having to adjust troublesome points). The clutch was a much lighter unit; it now had an aluminium basket, which was 7 mm larger than the GL1000's, with revised plates for greater strength. A new lever mechanism and rerouted cable made operating the clutch much easier and gave it a lighter feel. Four carburetors were still used. This time the size decreased from the K3/Z's 31 mm to 30 mm, and the upgraded aluminium Constant Velocity Keihin's were designed to give the GL1100 better low-end and mid-range response and featured an accelerator pump. The gear ratios were also slightly changed, with the secondary and final reductions altered along with second, third, fourth and fifth gears. The cooling system was the same as the GL1000's except for the redesigned water reservoir in the new faux tank. The radiator shrouds were larger and chrome-plated.

What was totally new, though, was the chassis; the tubular double cradle frame had been elongated to accommodate the new ignition system. The steering geometry was altered with the rake angle much steeper and a longer trail. The swingarm was also extended, making the wheelbase 1605 mm (63.2 inch). The suspension was new and all air-assisted; the two 39 mm fork legs (an increase of 2 mm from the GL1000) were connected, making air adjustment easier, as were the two VHD shock absorbers (all of this made the bike much more stable at higher speeds). This patented system had a low-pressure warning light in the tachometer that illuminated to indicate if the air pressure in the rear shock absorbers had dropped below 28 psi. Included in the bike's tool kit was a new tyre-pressure gauge, which made checking the tyres and suspension much easier. The wheels were now tubeless ComStars, with the steel spokes inverted and fixed to an aluminium rim. The spokes and rim edges were natural colours, with the rest of the wheel painted black. The front tyre size increased to a 110/90-H19, with the rear unaltered. Front and rear tyres became Dunlop Gold Seal F11 and K127 respectively. The front brakes were still the same as the CBX with the single-piston caliper, and Honda also redesigned the rear caliper to a single-piston unit.

The styling of the bike was more in keeping with the new custom sector of motorcycling with its tear-drop faux tank (now redesigned so only the top section opened in two parts making carrying a tank bag easier), stepped King and Queen seat, more enclosed front mudguard and pulled back handlebars featuring black bar ends. The instruments were more compact than before, with the centre light console now having the temperature and fuel gauges above them. Due to the new frame, the seat height decreased to 31.3 inches (795 mm). The seat itself could be adjusted 1.5 inches (40 mm) forward and backwards in three positions, but did require tools to do so. Touring range improved with a larger fuel tank capacity increasing two-tenths of a gallon to 4.4 Imp Gals (20 litres). The new side covers reverted back to the shape of the GL1000K0/2 and featured new Gold Wing and eagle-like emblems; the eagle had a shield with 'GL 1100' in the centre. The faux-tank also had a new emblem, along with the new plastic front mudguard. This was a small rectangular emblem, which read 'GL'. All were green and gold, which just added a bit of class to Honda's flagship. With the use of more plastic the bike's weight decreased to 589 lbs (267 kg).

Bird's-eye view of the GL1100. (Peter Rakestrow)

The transistorised ignition with vacuum advance bolted to the rear of the engine. (Peter Rakestrow)

The lever fitted to the GL1100 models from 1981 and on allowed the rider to adjust the seat by 1½ ins (40 mm) to three positions. Note the spring. (Peter Rakestrow)

The GL1100 front air-valve with balance pipe. (Peter Rakestrow)

Honda's patented pressure equaliser valve for the rear suspension. (Peter Rakestrow)

The biggest thing for 1980, after Honda had seen and listened to its customers over the previous two years, was the introduction of their first production 'turn-key tourer', the GL1100 Gold Wing Interstate. This was the first time Honda had offered a bike kitted out with all you could want: a fairing, a luggage rack, panniers, top-box, front engine bars and rear crash-bars incorporating the pannier brackets. Magazines dubbed the new Interstate a turn-key tourer because everything could be opened with the ignition key. This certainly got the aftermarket industry worried because there had been talk that the standard Gold Wing could be discontinued.

Back in 1974 Honda had fitted a small nose fairing to two pre-production GL1000s at the Las Vegas dealer convention with the intention of marketing them. Honda even asked Craig Vetter of Vetter Corporation to get involved, which he agreed to, and soon afterwards they sent him the drawings. Craig produced fifty fairings for Honda, which they duly advertised in 'THE HONDA REPORT' advert in magazines in 1975 as 'coming soon', but in the end they never marketed any of them. On some early GL1000 prototypes larger fairings were being made, but it wasn't until 1980 and the GL1100 that Honda decided to build a bike with one that was factory fitted. Honda did have concerns as to whether the fairing would affect the bike's handling. To reduce this concern they fitted a weight to the fork legs where the headlamp would normally mount, thus maintaining the big bike's stability. The fairing's polycarbonate screen was adjustable using tools, and Honda also fitted a hood to the instrument cluster to stop glare from them in the screen. Both the fairing and luggage were injection-moulded, made from acrylonitrile-butadiene-styrene (ABS) plastic. The fairing featured two air scoops with adjustable vents and had two storage pockets; one was lockable and the other had a press-stud vinyl cover. Honda fitted fairing-mounted mirrors similar to the ones used on their Civic car. The headlight was also adjustable using the knob behind the instruments. The design of the fairing was quite adaptive, Honda offering it as an option for the standard GL1100, but also for other motorcycles in their range. The concept of top and lower fairing parts came from Craig Vetter's own design with his Windjammer.

The luggage was well designed, the top-box being set low, and with its clamshell-type 49-litre capacity could accommodate two crash-helmets easily. When opened the lid would rest on the passenger seat. The box itself was quick-detachable using the ignition key and featured a carrying handle and internal mat. Passenger comfort was important so Honda incorporated a backrest on the top-box. The panniers had a capacity of 35 litres each and were top-loading units; they featured 'Interstate' emblems on the sides. Each pannier had two locks, one at either end, the only problem when you removed the lid was … where to put it so it didn't get damaged? The rear indicators were incorporated at the lower rear section of the pannier, making the whole package more integrated. Honda used the same lens as the ones fitted to the Civic car. Everything was colour matched to the bike and, for ease of packing, inner bags were standard equipment.

The Gold Wing's list of extras had grown. Not only could the GL1100 standard be turned into an Interstate but even more items could be added: for example, the Clarion AM/FM Type 1 stereo system that also had an intercom facility. Another option was an instrumentation panel designed to fit four gauges: a quartz clock, thermometer, voltmeter and altimeter.

Above: A GL1100IA Interstate, first available in the USA in March 1980. (Peter Rakestrow)

Right: Front mudguard in 1980/1, with Candy Grandeur Blue Special paint, gold stripe and the green 'GL' emblem. (Peter Rakestrow)

The fairing instrument panel, standard on the European models, with its voltmeter and clock. Note the headlight adjuster knob underneath them and optional Clarion speakers. The cowl over the instruments was to stop night-time glare in the windscreen. (Peter Rakestrow)

The GL1100 adjustable fairing vent and right-hand lockable pocket. (Peter Rakestrow)

Right: The left-hand vinyl push-stud covered pocket. This is where the optional cassette tape player would fit. The cover below this is where the AM/FM radio would fit. (Peter Rakestrow)

Below: Candy Grandeur Blue Special, sold in European markets but not the UK. (Peter Rakestrow)

45

While all of this sounded great, the UK market missed out a bit; although Honda (UK) did import both models, the Standard GL1100 being available in December 1979 and priced a little higher than the GL1000Z at £2,399, the Interstate (Deluxe in the UK) was not a complete bike – where was the luggage? This seemed to be the case across Europe. The bikes arrived with only the fairing and engine-guards, plus handlebar-mounted mirrors, although a fairing-mounted clock and voltmeter came as standard, though it was an option in the USA. The Deluxe first appeared on the 1 May 1980 price list with a RRP of £2,645. The luggage was eventually offered by Honda (UK) as an option at a cost of about £300; the reason Honda (UK) gave at the time for not supplying a complete bike was that they thought the price might be prohibitive. The Standard and Deluxe had long rear mudguards and flat handlebars (although not as flat as those on the GL1000). Three colour options were available for 1980: black, Candy Muse Red and Candy Grandeur Blue Special. The UK market received both models in the Candy Muse Red, while the European market was offered the Candy Grandeur Blue Special. All colours had gold striping.

At the time Gold Wings weren't one of Honda (UK)'s biggest sellers, but, with Honda offering a better package, enthusiasm was growing. Unbeknown to them, on 17 May 1980 a chap called Harry Ward had got together a small group of people at the Tower House Hotel in Reading for an inaugural meeting to form a new Gold Wing club in Britain. On that day the Gold Wing Club of Great Britain (GWCGB) had been formed by the thirty-seven riders who attended. Harry got straight to work and people flocked to join. One of his first jobs was to establish a relationship with Honda; he liaised with them to voice members' concerns regarding the Gold Wing and the club also pushed for the fully loaded Deluxe model to be brought into the UK.

The GL1100's much more comfortable stepped seat (King and Queen) with passenger backrest. The top-box was designed to be removable with the ignition key. Note the carrying handle on the lid. (Peter Rakestrow)

Honda GL500 Silver Wing, designed as the Gold Wing owner's partner's bike! (Peter Rakestrow)

In America the Gold Wing Interstate was so well received by customers and journalists alike that US publication *Cycle World* awarded the GL1100 Gold Wing Interstate the 'Best Touring Bike' title as it had done in 1977; however, this time it would keep it for the next couple of years.

1981 GL1100B and GL1100IB Interstate

Every year since its inception Honda had tweaked the Gold Wing, and the 1981 models were no exception. The Interstate became a huge worldwide success, with Honda selling its planned production in no time at all after its introduction in the States in March 1980. Gold Wing production had now been moved to America, where Honda started to produce the 1981 models in May 1980 at their new factory near Marysville, Ohio, although the engines still came from Japan at that time.

The tweaks started with the front mudguard, which now had a flared section at the lower rear. Honda had found on the 1980 models that the mudguard would flex at speed; the lower part could, and did, hit the tyre and break. The instrumentation was improved with a smooth plastic screen over the lights for better night-time illumination and a much cleaner look. Some customers complained that their GL1100's rear suspension bottomed-out when loaded with the recommended air pressure, so Honda increased the maximum air-pressure from 42 psi to 57 psi, which slightly improved the situation. Having an adjustable seat was a great idea, but having to get the tool kit out to do so was a bit of a chore. Honda made it a bit easier by fitting an automotive-type latch system with a spring, which just pulled out to move the seat to one of three positions, releasing the lever to secure it. In doing away with the handle-bar grips and bar ends from last year's model, Honda went back to the parts bin and used the same grips and chrome ends that were first used on the GL1000K2. The Gold Wing Interstate shared the same improvements, with the addition of a new anti-scratch coated polycarbonate windscreen.

This year the UK were spoilt a bit with Honda (UK) importing three models of the Gold Wing: the Standard GL1100B, the Deluxe GL1100DB and the Deluxe (special) GL1100DXB, as they called it. The DXB was the complete bike, with only 150 units imported, priced at £3,238, making the top-box, panniers, rack and rear crash-bars a bargain at £150. Honda imported the DXB to satisfy the pressure from the GWOCGB and it sold out within weeks. To distinguish between the Interstate and a Deluxe (special) DXB model, Honda replaced the 'Interstate' emblems on the panniers with 'Honda' ones. The GL1100DB was priced at £3,088 (fairing, instruments and engine-bars), with the Standard going for £2,688.

Colour choice in 1981 was a bit boring with Honda selling similar colours to the previous year: Candy Muse Red and a new Cosmo Black Metallic-U were available in the US, both on the Standard and Interstate models. Each had orange and gold striping. In Europe, however, it did get confusing. Both the Candy Muse Red and the Candy Grandeur Blue Special continued, but with the same gold striping as the year before. This caused a problem when certain spare painted parts were required; ordering from Honda (UK) the parts manual stated that the item was the same for the GL1100B/GL1100DB as the American GL1100IB Interstate, so when the part arrived it had the wrong colour stripe. It took some time for the parts manual to be corrected.

1981 GL1100DXB in Candy Muse Red, one of the original 150 units Honda UK imported as a complete package. This bike has had the same owner from new. (Peter Rakestrow)

GL1100AC Gold Wing Aspencade. The first time Honda had used two-tone paintwork on a Gold Wing. Sorrel Brown Metallic-U with Harvest Gold Metallic-U panels. Pictured at the GWOCGB Treffen in Beaulieu, Hampshire, in 1982. (Peter Rakestrow)

With the success of the GL1100 Gold Wing Interstate, Honda decided to offer a smaller capacity touring machine: the GL500 Silver Wing. The idea was that instead of husband and wife or partners travelling together on one machine, they could have two – a good marketing ploy! The GL500 was based more on the CX500 Custom than the standard CX500 in its design, and was fitted with the same top-half fairing as the GL1100. In Canada and America it also came with CBX-B style panniers and, to make the whole thing complete, Honda called the faired version an 'Interstate'. The optional stereo and instruments that fitted the fairing of the GL1100 also fitted the GL500, making the whole package, just with a smaller engine.

1982 GL1100C, GL1100IC Interstate and GL1100AC Aspencade (Project MB9)

Entering its eighth model year, and the penultimate one for the GL1100, the evolution continued, with even more improvements. This time the engine got a look-in as third, fourth and fifth gear ratios were higher, with the final reduction being lowered. This reduced the rpm at cruising speeds and improved fuel consumption. Honda moved the neutral switch, which had always lived behind the right-hand lower frame-member. If the switch packed up it was a near engine-out job to replace it; this was now relocated to behind the water-pump housing. One major noticeable difference was the wheels; although still ComStars, they got smaller and the tyres got bigger, with the front increasing to 120/90-18 and the rear to 140/90-16. Tyre life was also extended. Interestingly, this had the effect of reducing the bike's ground clearance by a quarter-inch (5 mm) and also reduced the overall length of the bike. To cope with the larger front tyre Honda made the mudguard wider. New twin-piston calipers and lighter front discs improved braking over previous models; the discs were the same as those first used on the 1981 CB400T. Improved switchgear incorporating self-cancelling indicators was fitted – a Honda first. The self-cancelling system was more compact than the one used on the 1974 pre-production GL1000, with a small computer sensing the fork's turning angle, speed and distance. If the fork is turned 2 degrees or more, then centred again, the canceller activates, taking into consideration time and distance travelled.

For lane changes, push the switch halfway, manoeuvre, and release the switch for it to cancel and return to the centre position. Honda again changed the handlebar grips with a new shape design; this made the grip more comfortable. The passenger foot-pegs were also redesigned, making them larger and softer, and, with Gold Wing owners fitting more and more electrical equipment to the bikes, Honda doubled the accessory terminals power output by uprating it to a 10-amp capacity.

The CBX-style ventilated discs with twin-piston calipers on the Aspencade. (Peter Rakestrow)

Rear passenger storage pockets in two-tone vinyl to match the seat on the Aspencade. (Peter Rakestrow)

The Clarion Type II radio with optional CB radio and intercom. (Peter Rakestrow)

Handlebar controls for the stereo system and CB radio. Tune (auto-seek) and mute buttons for the AM/FM stereo along with talk and channel change down/up buttons for the CB radio. (Peter Rakestrow)

The Interstate improvements resulted in the engine bars being redesigned following a lot of complaints from customers and the press alike; it was all too easy for the rider's shin to accidentally come into contact with the bars when stopping. Honda remedied this by shaping the lower part of the bar more towards the front of the engine, but this did not make too much difference. The panniers got improved weather seals to keep the inside drier, as some owners encountered water penetration on earlier models. By splitting the mudguard into two sections on the Interstate, and new Aspencade models, Honda made life a bit simpler when changing the rear tyre: by lifting the number plate holder, which was hinged, undoing two bolts, one on either side, and removing the lower section, getting the wheel out was made easier. The 1982 Gold Wing's emblems had the colour changed to black, whereas the previous year's had been green.

European customers didn't have the luxury and benefits of all the changes for 1982. The tyre sizes were still the same as before and the Deluxe model (still without panniers) didn't qualify for the rear mudguard changes. Some European markets were still offering the colour of Candy Grandeur Blue Special, while the UK got the new Candy Wineberry Red-U for both the Standard and Deluxe models. In America they continued with black and Cosmo Black Metallic-U, with the addition of Candy Wineberry Red-U.

Now with three models in the line-up, Honda upped the ante on 'luxury' by offering the Gold Wing-buying public the chance to own the most luxurious Gold Wing to date – the GL1100AC Gold Wing Aspencade. HAM's internal magazine *WING* reported that, 'As part of the Aspencade introduction, 3,000 American Honda dealers, guests and media visit HAM during the 1982 National Dealer Convention held in Columbus Sept. 20.'

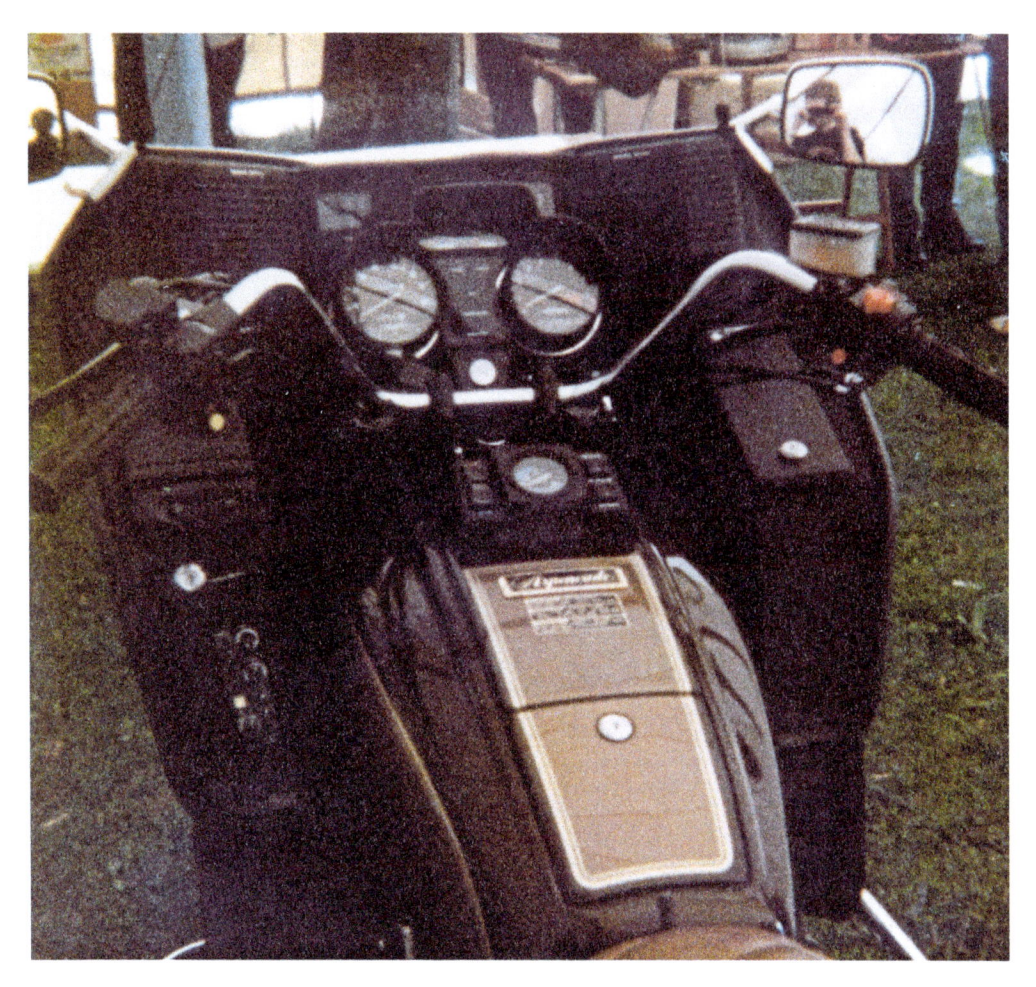

The 1982 Aspencade. Note the suspension adjustment system on the faux tank and the standard AM/FM type II radio on the left. (Peter Rakestrow)

The Gold Wing Aspencade was named after a large annual touring bike rally in the US. The Aspencade Rally started in 1971 and was held in Ruidoso, New Mexico, and was itself named after an annual civic festival celebrating the changing colours of the aspen (birch) trees. In May 1983 Aspencade East was founded in Lake George, New York, by veteran motorcycle racer Bill Dutcher and his wife Gini, with help from Til Thompson, who founded the original rally. In 1986 Aspencade East became Americade.

The Aspencade was the first Gold Wing to have two-tone paint work, with two colourways offered: Sorrel Brown metallic with Harvest Gold metallic panels and gold pinstripe, and Sterling Silver metallic with Tempest Gray metallic panels, also with gold pinstripe. The seat, 'the deepest, plushest, seat on two wheels' according to the American sales brochure, and the larger passenger backrest with new passenger top-box mounted side pockets were all two-tone vinyl. Inside the top-box there was a vanity mirror and map case located in the lid and a quilted floor liner. The soft convenient luggage bags were again standard but sported new Aspencade logos.

For the first time as standard equipment, a new Clarion AM/FM Type II stereo radio was included, which came complete with waterproof stereo speakers, handlebar-mounted controls and antenna; its digital readout for the channels, located in the fairing meter panel along with the voltmeter, doubled up as a clock. Also available as optional extras were forty-channel CB, intercom and cassette deck.

The brake-discs fitted to the front and rear on the '82 Aspencade were CBX-B type, internally-ventilated disc brakes with dual-piston calipers. The weight had increased to 702 lbs dry (compared to the Gold Wing Interstate's 679 lbs dry).

Luxury didn't stop at the overall appearance of the bike: it extended to the tool kit and leather-bound owner's manual as well. The tool kit contained fully chromed tools with spanners, adjustable spanner (monkey wrench), pliers and a set of sockets with ratchet. All were presented in a leather tool roll and stored in a plastic tool tray in the right-hand pannier.

The feature that really made the '82 Aspencade special was another motorcycling first, an on-board air compressor system with built-in pressure gauge. This was mounted on top of the front faux tank panel with the compressor inside the faux tank; the four buttons were front, rear, increase and decrease, so it could increase/decrease the suspension in the front fork or rear shock absorbers. The system could only be operated when the bike was stationary and on the centre stand, with the ignition in the 'P' position; the owner's manual stated that the suspension should be cold.

GL1100AC Gold Wing Aspencade's compressor components. Note the unique tank top emblem. (Peter Rakestrow)

Luxury always come at a price and, in the States, the Aspencade retailed for $6,798, which was $1,350 more than the Interstate. The 1982 Aspencade was officially limited to two countries only, the USA and Canada and, as the American sales brochure states: 'Now you know how the man who bought the first Rolls-Royce felt. A machine as dedicated to luxury on two wheels as the Rolls-Royce is dedicated to luxury on four.'

Harry Ward, the driving force behind the GWOCGB and its management committee were disappointed that Honda (UK) weren't bringing the Aspencade into Britain for 1982 due to the depressed state of the motorcycle market. The club eventually persuaded Honda to bring one in to promote it, which they duly did, displaying a two-tone Sorrel Brown Metallic Aspencade at the club's main event of the year, the British International Treffen in July at Beaulieu. This gave club members an early scoop, even seeing it before the motorcycle press. In the August edition of the club magazine *WingSpan,* a questionnaire was included to see who would be interested in the Aspencade. The following month the results were published, with 6 per cent of members responding saying they would buy the Aspencade at a cost of £4,250 if the AM/FM radio was fitted.

1983 GL1100D, GL1100ID Interstate and GL1100AD Aspencade

Honda had been developing a program of 'V4' configuration powered motorcycles for some time and started by launching the V45 Magna and Sabre models in America during 1981. Rumours kept appearing in the motorcycle press about the Gold Wing's replacement; in *M.C.N.* 1 September 1982 they reported 'HONDA TO LAUNCH V6', a 1300cc V6 Gold Wing.

The competition: Yamaha with their XVZ1200TD. Launched as a 1983 model and updated to a 1300cc model in 1986. Originally sold in the USA in two versions and sold in the UK in 1985. The Yamaha survived for ten years. (Peter Rakestrow)

A rare US-specification 1983 GL1100 AD Gold Wing Aspencade in a late-production colour, Sorrel Brown Metallic-U. (Peter Rakestrow)

The author's 1983 US-specification GL1100D. (Peter Rakestrow)

This speculation proved to be well wide of the mark! The GL1100 Gold Wing was showing signs of age and the competition was breathing down its neck yet again, with two Japanese manufacturers, Yamaha and Kawasaki, closing in fast. Yamaha's new V4 1200cc Venture Royale was a more powerful and better-handling bike, Kawasaki on the other hand, launched a six-cylinder mega-tourer based on the Z1300 (with gadgets galore); the ZN1300 Voyager, a monstrous, overweight machine by anyone's standards. Honda kept improving the GL1100 but it wasn't enough as, although magazine comparison tests praised the Gold Wing, they came out in favour of the Yamaha for its handling and power.

Improvements this year were exceptional, with new aesthetically pleasing eleven-spoke cast wheels, gone were the ComStars ... or were they? The suspension was considerably uprated; the front forks were still 39 mm, but now incorporated Honda's Torque Reactive Anti-Dive Control (TRAC). The system was designed to stop forward weight transfer when braking. There was a four-position adjuster in each leg to vary the anti-dive effect. The fork legs were also stiffened with an integrated fork brace. At the rear, the shock absorbers were uprated so they could now run without air. The engine also saw more improvements, with the left-hand engine casing recast for the much larger oil inspection window. The gearbox was tinkered with by increasing the secondary reduction and lowering first gears ratio, which reduced the rpm at cruising speeds – at 60 mph the engine was now only turning at 3,100 rpm. The light for the air suspension in the tachometer (on the Standard and Interstate) was now used to indicate 'over-drive' as the rear suspension didn't need any low-pressure warning light anymore. Operation of the choke was made easier with a lever; it was relocated (due to the Aspencade's new instrumentation) and incorporated into the clutch lever bracket. As Honda wanted the Gold Wing to appeal to the Americans as an American-built machine, they also took 'Made in Japan' off the rocker-box covers.

The 1983 model with Torque Reactive Anti-Dive Control (TRAC). Eleven-spoke cast wheels were fitted to US and Canadian models with Dunlop Qualifier tyres as standard. (Peter Rakestrow)

Left: The GL1100 differential and rear air shock absorbers. (Peter Rakestrow)

Below: GL1100s in 1983 had the choke lever moved because of the Aspencade's new LCD instrumentation. (Peter Rakestrow)

The 1983 model's larger rider foot pegs. The Interstate/Deluxe and Aspencade's passenger foot-pegs were adjustable. (Peter Rakestrow)

Honda had a problem on the 1982 Aspencade model with the 'pin bolt', which prompted a product update to be resolved under warranty. The left front disc was susceptible to uneven wear and the pin bolt caused pressure to build up and stopped the caliper returning to its neutral position. For 1983 Honda decided to use the heavier and more robust front discs from the CB900F on both the Standard and Interstate; the Aspencade, however, had redesigned ventilated front discs and a solid rear. The braking system itself was new – the 1983 GL1100 series was the first Honda street bike to come with a linked braking system, which Honda called 'Unified Braking'. This system derived from a 'works' RCB1000 race-bike, which had won numerous endurance race victories in 1976. When riding a motorcycle with a conventional braking system, the rider would tend to use more front brake than rear; with the 'Unified Braking' system the rider needs to use more rear pedal than front lever because the right-hand front and the rear brake operate together via a proportioning valve, while the front lever operates only the left-hand front brake. Also this year rider and passenger comfort was improved, with much wider foot pegs with chrome bases.

The Interstate and Aspencade followed on with small changes; the engine bars were totally redesigned and strengthened, and they now sat closer to the rocker-box covers. The ergonomics experts at Honda had been busy fine-tuning the rear accommodation; the top-box was situated an inch (25 mm) higher and was moved back 1.2 inch (30 mm) just to give the passenger more space behind the rider. The backrest on the top-box of the Interstate was now the same size as the Aspencade's and, along with the seat, was made

A UK-specification 1983 GL1100AD Gold Wing Aspencade in Nimbus Grey Metallic-U. Note the ComStar wheels. The owner has fitted the fairing-mounted mirrors. Only 150 were imported by Honda UK. (Peter Rakestrow)

The most advanced instrumentation yet was fitted to the 1983 Aspencade – liquid crystal display with compressor and trip controls. This UK bike has the optional Type 1 stereo radio fitted. (Peter Rakestrow)

in a different single-coloured vinyl complementing the bike's main colour. Seating on the Aspencade had been redesigned from the previous year's with the rider's lumber section 1.2 inches (30 mm) narrower and it had been reduced in height; the seat style on the Interstate was now the same as the Aspencade's. The rear crash bars were extended on the lower fixing point so the passenger foot-rests could be adjusted to one of two positions.

Technology was moving at a rapid pace in the automotive world with the use of LCD instrumentation and Honda were also trying it out on motorcycles. The Aspencade was the first Gold Wing to use liquid crystal display (LCD) instrumentation; the bike's information centre had just gone into the stratosphere. The beautifully shaped oval consul provided fuel, temperature, rpm (in bar and digit formats), speedometer and trip-meter information along with the normal warning/information lights. Two new features were a gear indicator, which was very welcome, and what Honda called 'a special maintenance indicator', which was situated beneath the analogue six-digit odometer. The Gold Wing's service intervals had been extended; the service indicator would be green up to 8,000 miles, then turning yellow and, when the bike reached 9,000 miles, it turned red. This could be reset by inserting the ignition key into the slot below the service indicator. The instrumentation features were abundant; changing from mph to kph could be achieved at the touch of a button and the compressor controls had been moved to just below the instruments, freeing-up the faux tank again. Pushing the front or rear suspension selector button changed the temperature gauge to an air-pressure gauge. The previous year Honda had added self-cancelling turn signals and, for 1983, they were improved using the same system as the V45 Sabre's, which relied more on speed and distance rather than steering deflection. Honda found that, if the steering wasn't deflected enough, the turn-signals wouldn't cancel.

In Britain Honda answered the GWOCGB's prayers by importing just the Aspencade model for 1983, as they still had plenty of GL1100Cs in stock. 150 units were provided at a cost of £4,250 each; they sold out within two months. Although the bike was complete with luggage and was the new model, the look of the bike was still old, with handlebar-mounted mirrors and 19-inch and 17-inch ComStar wheels (not gone after all then!), but at least it had the higher, more comfortable handlebars fitted. One other thing Honda (UK) did offer as an option was the Clarion Type 1 radio and intercom system, complete with fairing-mounted speakers and antenna. This cost an extra £253.

During a meeting the GWOCGB had with Honda (UK) about the future of the Gold Wing in this country, I posed the question to their PR officer at the time: 'Why don't Honda import Gold Wings with fairing-mounted mirrors?' The answer was simple: 'They don't conform to UK regulations'; my response to that was, 'How come the GL500 Silver Wing had them fitted then, as it is the same fairing top as the GL1100?' This was met with silence. Let's move on ...

Colour choice in the UK for the Aspencade was limited to two-tone Nimbus Grey Metallic-U. Although three colour choices in the USA were available, the sales brochures and American Honda's marketing information only mentions two. This was also the case with the Interstate. The other colours were two-tone Candy Wineberry Red-U and a late-produced Sorrel Brown Metallic-U (same as the 1982 Aspencade). Colour choice for the Standard GL1100 went back to darker colours, with the options being black or Candy Regal Brown. Interstate colours were the same as the Standard, but with the addition of a late-produced Candy Wineberry Red-U.

A German-registered GL1100DC with every conceivable chrome extra fitted. In Britain the law to allow towing trailers was changed in 1984. (Peter Rakestrow)

Specifications

GL1100 1980–1983
Dimensions
Overall length	STD	2,345 mm (92.3 inches) [2,355 mm (92.7 inches)]
	STD ('82/'83)	2,340 mm (92.1 inches)
	INT/Deluxe	2,405 mm (94.7 inches) [2,355 mm (92.7 inches)]
	INT ('82)	2,400 mm (94.7 inches)
	ASP ('82)	2,430 mm (95.6 inches)
	INT/ASP ('83)	2,460 mm (96.9 inches)
Overall width		920 mm (36.2 inches) [825 mm (32.5 inches)]
Overall height	STD	1,195 mm (47.0 inches) [1,160 mm (45.7 inches)]
	INT/Deluxe	1,500 mm (59.1 inches) [1,500 mm (59.1 inches)]
	INT/ASP ('82/'83)	1,495 mm (58.9 inches)** [1,500 mm (59.1 inches)]*

Wheel base		1,605 mm (63.2 inches)
Ground clearance		145 mm (5.7 inches)
	STD/INT/ASP ('82/'83)	140 mm (5.5 inches)**

Weight

Dry weight	STD ('80/'81)	267 kg (589 lbs) ('83) 272 kg (600 lbs)
	INT/Deluxe ('80/'81)	305 kg (672 lbs) [285 kg (628 lbs)]
	STD ('82)	270 kg (595 lbs)
	INT/Deluxe ('82)	308 kg (679 lbs) [285 kg (628 lbs)] ('83) 311 kg (686 lbs)
	ASP ('82)	318.5 Kg (702 lbs) ('83) 321 kg (708 lbs) [317kg (699lbs)]

Engine

Bore and stroke	75.0 × 61.4 mm (2.95 × 2.42 inches)
Compression ratio	9.2:1
Displacement	1,085cc (66.2 cu-in)
Carburetors	4 × 30 mm CV Keihin
Power output	83 bhp @ 7,500 rpm

Power transmission		1980/'81	1982	1983
Primary reduction		1.708	1.708	1.708
Secondary reduction		0.973	0.973	0.897
Gear Ratio	1st.	2.500	2.500	2.643
	2nd.	1.667	1.667	1.667
	3rd.	1.286	1.250	1.250
	4th.	1.065	1.000	1.000
	5th.	0.909	0.829	0.829
Final reduction		3.091	3.100	3.100

Chassis and suspension

Castor	60 degrees 50 minutes
Trail	132 mm (5.2 inches)
Tyre size	Front ('80/'81) 110/90-19 62H Tubeless [110/90-19 62H Tubeless]****
	Rear ('80/'81) 130/90-17 68H Tubeless [130/90-17 68H Tubeless]****
	Front ('82/'83) 120/90-18 65H Tubeless
	Rear ('82/'83) 140/90-16 71H Tubeless

Electrical

Battery	12v – 20AH
Generator output	300 watt @ 5,000 rpm A.C. Three phase

Notes: [ ] UK type. *Aspencade only. **USA and Canadian models only. ****UK type 1980–1983.

4

Greater Heights for Honda's Flagship

1984 GL1200E, GL1200IE Interstate and GL1200AE Aspencade (Project MG9)

Commanding only 23 per cent of the market share, Harley-Davidson, the last surviving American motorcycle manufacturer, had hit hard times as far as sales were concerned, with Honda holding on to 45 per cent. The US President at the time, Ronald Reagan, took the unprecedented step in April 1983 to protect Harley by increasing the 'import tariff' tenfold from 4.4 per cent to 49.4 per cent, scaled back over five years. This didn't really affect the Gold Wing, as it was built in the USA anyway, and Harley's tourers weren't in the same league as the Gold Wing, nor were they as sophisticated as the Japanese machines in general.

Honda's CX500 Turbo was instrumental in the GL1200's fairing design. This image was captured at a Bonham's auction in Stafford. (Peter Rakestrow)

The Gold Wing was the 'bench mark standard' against which all others were judged; unfortunately the competition, especially the other Japanese companies, were getting a little too close and the standard needed to improve. With Honda being the world's number one motorcycle manufacturer, they obliged. Following the advent of 'turbo-charged' Japanese bikes a couple of years earlier, such as Yamaha's XJ650T and Suzuki's XN85, Honda decided to model the third-generation Gold Wing with a more aggressive look. The fairing and headlamp took some design cues from their own CX500 Turbo. Launched in Europe at the Milan Motorcycle Show, Italy, late in 1983, the GL1200 Gold Wing was totally revised and came as a complete package for European markets. Although most of its parts had been redesigned and the dimensions increased, the basic architecture of the Gold Wing engine again remained the same.

Over the next four years the Gold Wing struggled to maintain its lead over the competition. Some American magazines such as *Rider* loved the Gold Wing; in June 1983 they dedicated virtually the whole magazine to the Gold Wing, with road tests on the Standard and Aspencade, saying, 'It has become the role model for big, fully equipped touring machines'. *Road Rider* magazine's editors Bob and Patti Carpenter, on the other hand, fell in love with the Yamaha and took it on a six-month road test, covering over 50,000 miles across forty-nine states in America, including Alaska and all twelve Canadian provinces, to evaluate it.

Honda needed to do something to regain its title as 'Best Touring Bike' but, with the launch of Yamaha's Venture Royale the year earlier, was this new GL1200 enough? *Rider* magazine's last words in a test on the new Yamaha Venture Royale in their May 1983 issue were, 'The new era is upon us'. The Gold Wing has the best-designed engine for a

The 1984 GL1200E Standard Gold Wing was only built for one year and in a small quantity due to lack of sales. (Peter Rakestrow)

A 1984 UK-specification GL1200DE Deluxe. Note the handlebar-mounted mirrors. (Peter Rakestrow)

touring bike – it's smooth, well balanced and keeps the centre of gravity low, unlike some competitors. V4 and in-line six-cylinders like Yamaha's and Kawasaki's are set higher in their frames. The only downside to the opposed configuration engine in the Gold Wing was ground clearance when cornering.

In 1984 the challenge was on for Honda to improve the Gold Wing far beyond what it had been before. How could they turn a heavyweight 778 lbs (353 kg) kerb weight Gold Wing Aspencade into a machine that handled like a 600cc motorcycle? When Honda started to design what was to become the GL1200, they visited motorcycle rallies in the US and asked customers about different engine configurations. The response was that, if it had a different engine configuration, it wouldn't be a Gold Wing! So Honda took this on board and designed a new bike that still looked like a Gold Wing but, by repositioning the engine and fitting smaller wheels and huge tyres, it became a better handling bike with much quicker steering. Bingo – they amazed everyone with what they achieved.

Honda offered three different models in Canada and America: the Standard, Interstate and Aspencade. The GL1200's 1182cc horizontally opposed engine still had two valves per cylinder and toothed rubber belts, the bore had increased to 75.5 mm and the stroke to 66 mm. The engine produced 13 per cent more torque than the GL1100 at 77.2 lbs ft at 5,500 rpm and 94 bhp at 7,000 rpm. It also came with more maintenance-free items such as a hydraulic clutch. Valve adjustment was now a thing of the past with Honda incorporating hydraulic tappets into the larger cylinder heads for the first time. To boost power they made the intake valve smaller and reduced the size of the combustion chamber, improving the squish area. The redesigned Keihin carburetors, which reverted back to the original GL1000 32 mm size, featured Hydron diaphragm throttle valves that were designed to give better economy and respond quickly to intake vacuum changes; these were fed via an electric fuel pump that replaced the old mechanical unit on the previous models. The carburettors gave the top of the engine a different look and shape from the older models.

The GL1200's engine with redesigned carburettors and rocker-box covers. (Peter Rakestrow)

The electric fuel pump, with the engine oil filler cap and oil dip-stick below. (Peter Rakestrow)

The GL1200E with analogue instrumentation similar to the GL1100s, also with a unique faux tank emblem. (Peter Rakestrow)

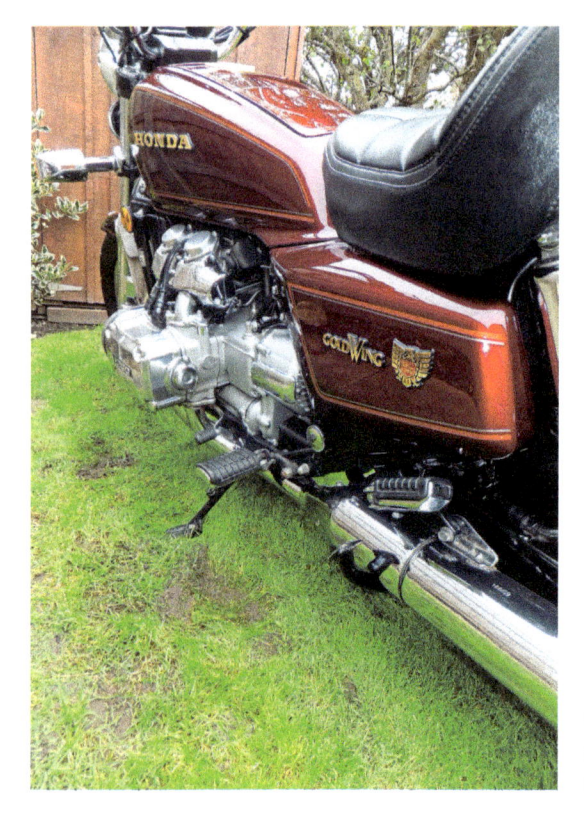

The redesigned GL1200 side cover with new emblems now flow into the faux tank. (Peter Rakestrow)

The GL1200 faux tank opens in two halves. Note the securing latch for the front half. The tool tray for storing the toolkit in its roll. Also seen are two owner's manuals: the red one is for the Canadian market in French and English, the other for the US market. (Peter Rakestrow)

One problem with the Gold Wing has always been its fuel range. Due to where the fuel tank is situated under the seat, it is difficult to increase the capacity but, with the newly designed GL1200, Honda managed to increase the tank capacity to 4.8 Imp gal (22 litres). A much larger plenum chamber under the air-filter box helped the GL1200 breathe more quietly and added to engine pickup response. The chassis, again, was all new with weight distribution altered; to achieve this Honda moved the engine 2.5 inches (63.5 mm) forward and tilted it up 3 degrees. This in turn gave the rider more leg room and improved ground clearance when cornering. Weight distribution was better balanced with 44 per cent at the front and 56 per cent at the rear. Honda redesigned the GL1200's radiator for more efficient cooling by making it a smaller two-core unit and the coolant capacity had also been reduced. With the increased electronics on the bikes Honda increased the alternator output to 360 watts at 5,000 rpm. Another feature of the GL1200's engine was easier oil checks, which were achieved by discarding the oil sight window and replacing it with a dip-stick instead.

The GL1200's frame had been lengthened along with the swingarm, which in turn increased the wheelbase slightly by one quarter-inch (5 mm). The seat height had been reduced to 30.7 inch (780 mm); on paper this should have been better for riders who had short inseams. Instead they found that the frame at that point widened so the distance to

A UK-specification GL1200DE Deluxe, with the 'Gold Wing' rear light signature. (Peter Rakestrow)

the floor wasn't much better. The steering geometry was altered, with the rake decreased by 0.833 degrees and the trail shortened from 5.2 inches (132 mm) to 4.6 inches (118 mm). Front fork stanchions increased 2 mm in size to 41 mm for greater strength and to help with the increased forward engine weight. Honda also redesigned the lower fork-leg and TRAC system. All the suspension remained air-assisted, which gave a better and much smoother ride. Exhaust tone was slightly altered from the GL1100 with a redesigned exhaust system; interestingly, Honda reverted back to a large one-piece 'U' shaped silencer similar to that on the original GL1000. The all-chromed system featured oval tail-pipes on the Interstate and Aspencade, which gave the rear of the bike a more attractive look.

Wheel and tyre sizes on motorcycles were becoming unconventional at this time with smaller front wheels and larger rear ones; the GL1200's wheels got smaller but stayed the conventional way round. The wheels were a cast alloy, nine-spoke design, with the front being of a 16-inch diameter, carrying a 130/90-16 tyre. This was the same width and profile as the rear on the original GL1000. The rear shrunk to a 15-inch diameter wheel with a larger 150/90-15 tyre. With the front tyre being so big and the steering geometry changed, this gave the GL1200 much quicker and more sensitive steering, making the bike feel lighter than it really was; some owners didn't quite like it and preferred the heavier feel of the GL1100.

Integration was becoming part of motorcycle design, with the aim of making the machine look like one complete unit as opposed to looking like the fairing and luggage had been added afterwards. This was a feature of the Yamaha Venture Royale. With the Gold Wing Interstate and Aspencade, Honda made the faux tank flow into the fairing, which featured a flush-mounted adjustable rectangular headlamp with twin side lights. The new Type III Panasonic radio/auto-reverse cassette player (on the Aspencade) looked part of the 'automotive style' instrumentation, which was now incorporated into the fairing.

The Type III stereo system was 12 watts per channel, incorporated the intercom system and had an automatic volume control that adjusted to the speed of the motorcycle – a unique feature of the Type III system. The radio unit itself could be removed using the ignition key and to stop water ingress a blanking cover could be inserted in its place. Also, just below the speaker housings were new cool-air, flow-through adjustable vents. The panniers were integrated into the rear mudguard with rear light units being part of the luggage. The top-box featured a signature light-bar across its length with the machine's name across it: 'Aspencade', 'Interstate' or, for the European Deluxe model, 'Gold Wing'. Luggage capacity increased by 16.8 per cent to 139 litres with each pannier swallowing 38 litres of luggage, and two full-face helmets fitted in the 63-litre top-box with ease. The top-box was situated lower than before, but now wasn't detachable, though it incorporated a much larger passenger backrest. The lid was about fifty-fifty with the base, was clamshell-type and still featured two locks. Again, when opened the lid conveniently rested on the passenger seat. The new hump design in the lid incorporated an internal storage compartment on the Aspencade, complete with vanity mirror, an option on the Interstate. One other feature on the Aspencade model was the two passenger side pockets, which had longer solid tops and doubled up as armrests. The panniers still had locks on each end and were still top loading, but the lids had been reshaped, with the pannier opening angled for ease of loading. The luggage weatherproof seals were much improved, featuring lips inside with recessed rubber seals. Rider and passenger comfort was improved with a much wider and longer seat which, along with the passenger backrest, featured an embossed GL1200 emblem. It was still adjustable but via a more complex system, with the adjuster located in the faux tank behind the fuel filler cap. The Interstate and Aspencade both had side wind-tips added

The GL1200 Interstate/Deluxe and Aspencade's 38-litre top-loading panniers. (Peter Rakestrow)

The 'GAS' filler cap for the under-seat fuel tank. Also the more complicated seat adjuster lever on 1984 models. (Peter Rakestrow)

to the windscreen, which were secured by specially designed screw-on clips, making the windscreen much wider for added wind protection.

Instrumentation on all three models differed; the Standard model had similar analogue instruments to that of the GL1100, while the Interstate/Deluxe got an automotive style dashboard featuring analogue instruments, which included speedometer and new electronic tachometer. The radio and speaker compartments were blanked off. The stereo could be fitted as an option along with numerous other extras from Hondaline. The instruments on the Aspencade had warning and information lights down each side, while the centre console was an all-new LCD panel featuring larger digits. On the lower right side of the fairing were the air-pressure controls for the Aspencade's suspension compressor. One addition to the system was the inclusion of an outlet valve, which allowed owners to check and inflate tyres with the bike's compressor using the standard air hose supplied with the tool kit. With their top-of-the-line model Honda made the passenger even more comfortable by adding rear foot boards, which could be folded up out of the way when the bike was being put on the centre-stand.

American magazines took to the GL1200 straight away with the cover of the February 1984 issue of *Cycle* saying, 'HONDA GL1200 GOLD WING. Same Name, Same Dress, But ... A Whole New Bird'. *Cycle Canada*, in the same month, said in their road test of the Aspencade, 'INVISIBLY ENHANCED. The '84 Aspencade looks much the same. Don't be fooled', and Honda Canada headlined their Gold Wing advert, 'RULE THE ROUTES', with their slogan, 'HONDA THE REASON YOU RIDE'.

When the GL1200 arrived in the UK it was a pleasant surprise; with the exception again of the fairing-mounted mirrors, screen wind-tips and some lighting, the bikes were nearly the same as those for the American market. As with the GL1100 Aspencade before it, the UK-specification GL1200s came with the same high handlebars as the American bikes.

The Aspencade's comprehensive LCD instruments with Panasonic radio/cassette. Note the adjustable vents under the speakers and headlamp adjuster on the left. (Peter Rakestrow)

Without the fairing mirrors for protection one problem with having the high, pulled-back handlebars was that the rider's hands were exposed. Two models were available in the UK, the Deluxe and Aspencade, each in different colours. The GL1200DE was available in Senior Gray Metallic-U, with the GL1200AE in two-tone Premium Beige Metallic-U. Colour choices in America for the Standard model were Black-Z and Candy Wineberry Red-U, while three colours were offered for the Interstate: Pearl Siren Blue-A, Senior Gray Metallic-U and Wineberry Red-U. The Aspencade also had three colour options, in this case two-tone versions of Pearl Siren Blue-A, Pearl Saturn Red-A and Premium Beige Metallic-U.

At this time the Gold Wing's prices started to rise more steeply than had been seen previously, with the Deluxe coming in at £290 more than the 1983 GL1100 Aspencade at £4,540, while the new Aspencade retailed for a whopping £5,780.

Due to the integrated design of the GL1200, the options list had to be different; the Interstate/Aspencade fairing could not be fitted to the Standard model, although the panniers and top-box weren't a problem. To overcome this Honda adapted the GL1100 fairing instead, making different fairing lowers and bracket.

When the GL1200 was introduced Honda America decided to launch an owner's association called 'Wing Elite'; membership was free when you bought a new Gold Wing. It included personal membership cards and pins, as well as a quarterly magazine with features on travelling and tips about owning a Gold Wing.

1985 GL1200IF Interstate, GL1200AF Aspencade and GL1200LF Limited Edition

Since 1983 Honda had been redesigning major parts and must have been spending vast sums of money on the Gold Wing's development – in some cases, parts were only used for one model year. 1985 proved to be the turning point in the 'touring market'. The fears of the aftermarket fairing and saddlebag manufacturers came true as Honda decided to drop the Standard Gold Wing from their line-up; it was manufactured for one year only with a very small number built and sold.

With two of the Japanese motorcycle manufacturers already producing competition for the Gold Wing, Suzuki launched their own fully loaded touring bike, the GV1400 Cavalcade, a four-stroke liquid-cooled 82-degree V-4 with the double-overhead camshaft engine having four valves per cylinder. The wheelbase was very long at 65.7 inches (1,670 mm), 2.3 inches (58 mm) longer than the Gold Wing's. Not the heaviest of the four manufacturer's bikes, it still weighed in at 768 lbs (349 kg).

For 1985 Honda did some major redesigning of most of the GL1200. Both the Interstate and Aspencade saw engine changes and the electronic ignition was moved from the rear of the engine and now used pulse generators inside the cam-belt covers. The left belt cover was redesigned and made thinner, and the gear ratios were slightly higher for first and fifth gears. Although the Gold Wing's cooling system had been revised in 1984, Honda improved it further by redesigning the water pump. The pump had basically been the same since 1975 with its moulded Bakelite impeller; the improvement was to make the impeller out of steel instead, which in turn made the pump more efficient. Honda also revised the starter motor, making it a more substantial unit than before.

A 1985 GL1200AF Aspencade in Sandy Beige Metallic, complete with aftermarket exhaust extensions and rear light-bars. (Peter Rakestrow)

'Mission Control'. The 1985 GL1200LF Limited Edition in its two-tone Sunflash Gold Metallic paint work. (Peter Rakestrow)

Computerised fuel injection system on the 1985 GL1200 Limited Edition and 1986 GL1200SE-i. (Peter Rakestrow)

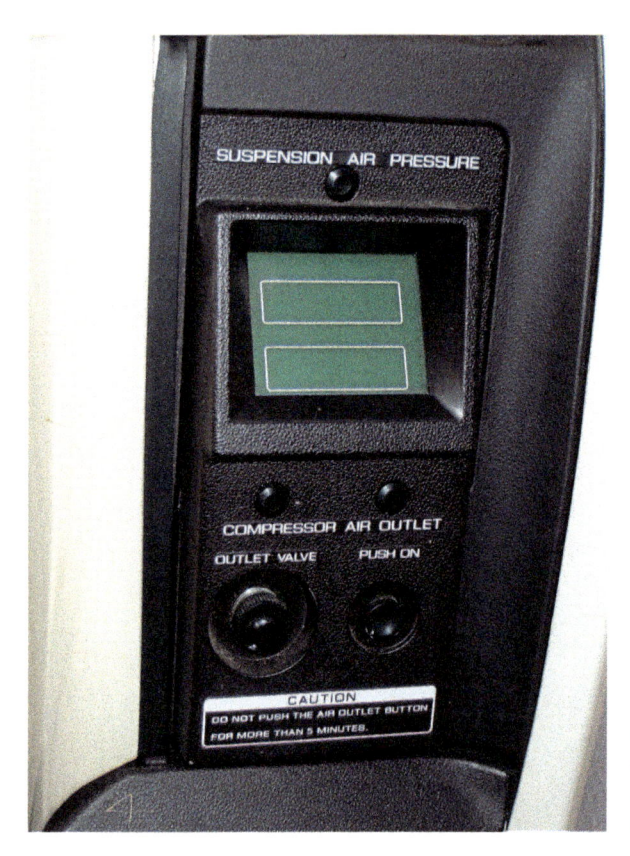

Suspension air-pressure gauge in the right-hand lower fairing on the 1985 GL1200 Limited Edition and 1986 GL1200SE-i. (Henning Kristiansen)

The controls for the Auto-Levelling-Rear-Suspension, along with the radio and CB switches on the 1985 GL1200 Limited Edition and 1986 GL1200SE-i. (Peter Rakestrow)

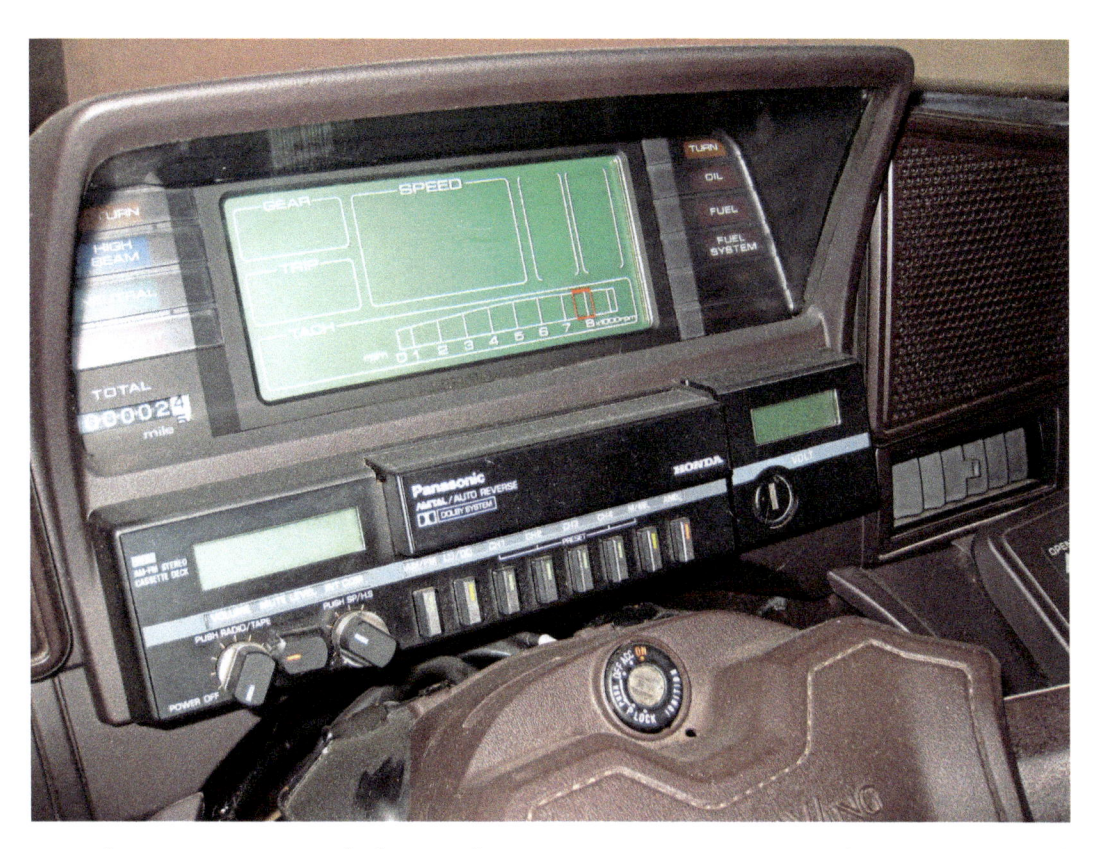

The 1985 GL1200 Limited Edition and 1986 GL1200SE-i instrumentation. (Henning Kristiansen)

The handlebars, along with the clamp cover and switchgear, were redesigned with the indicator switch now having a push-to-cancel feature. On the Aspencade the LCD instrumentation had a completely new look and the fairing mirrors were redesigned; they had also been raised up slightly, giving a better rear view. The seat was still adjustable to three positions but Honda decided to scrap the complicated system they had designed for the 1984 models and reverted back to the latch mechanism from the GL1100. The top-box rack incorporated grab-handles for the passenger; on the previous model they were just a bit too low, so Honda reshaped them. Another problem with the 1984 Interstate and Aspencade was that the luggage wasn't as integrated as first thought. In heavy rain spray from the rear wheel would come up between the pannier and the seat, getting the rider and passenger wet from behind. To overcome this Honda fitted splash guards to the underside of the rear mudguard.

The reason for so many changes after just one year in production was that Honda introduced the most technologically advanced Gold Wing to date, the GL1200LF Limited Edition. Mr Hideaki Nebu was head of development for the Limited Edition, saying it 'was instrumental in fortifying the Gold Wing series concept'. He had earlier contributed to the development of the GL1100. The bike was designed to celebrate two facts in American Honda's history, firstly the tenth anniversary of the Gold Wing and secondly the twenty-fifth anniversary of American Honda. In its design Mr Nebu wanted to use fuel-injection and a cruise control system, so the GL1200 LTD was the first Gold Wing to feature a Computerised-Fuel-Injection system. In developing the CFI Honda had problems with vapor-lock as the complex fuel system pipework and all the bodywork on the bike caused the fuel to rise in temperature, creating air bubbles that would stop fuel circulation. Mr Nebu said, 'After a lot of trial and error we thought we had sufficiently solved the problem, but after we released the GL1200 LTD we realised the actual usage was more severe than anticipated.' This issue would not be addressed until the following year. Mounted on the faux tank was the Electronic Travel Computer (originally to be called an Electronic Navigator), which featured a map of North America linked to the clock and split into six different time zones: Y = Alaskan Standard Time (AKST), P = Pacific (PST), M = Mountain (MST), C = Central (CST), E = Eastern (EST) and A = Atlantic (AST). These could be altered at the push of a button. Other functions were fuel consumption, how much fuel was left and how far could be travelled at the present rate before running out, average trip speed, elapsed time and total trip mileage. Some of the Aspencade's trip buttons located on the handlebar cover were moved on the LTD and incorporated into the ETC, along with the clock. In the clock's place, next to the radio unit, Honda fitted a voltmeter to keep an eye on the charging system, which had been increased to 490 watts at 5,000 rpm. The Limited's LCD instrument panel had more features, including a tachometer with digits and bar-graph. Two gauges were dual purpose: one combined coolant and oil temperature, the other fuel and oil pressure. Other electronic gadgets fitted were Auto-Levelling Rear Suspension (ALRS). The control levers were located above the left handlebar switch cluster with the readout being in the right-hand side of the lower fairing beneath the lockable pocket. In the lower left side of

Emblems and owner's manuals for the 1985 Limited Edition and 1986 Aspencade SE-i. Also the LTD embossed owner's certificate. (Peter Rakestrow)

the fairing Honda incorporated a small pullout pocket designed to store cassette tapes. New rear passenger speakers fitted to the top-box lid were controlled by a joystick arrangement in the ETC, moving the sound from speaker to speaker. Mr Nebu wanted to incorporate electronic cruise-control technology into the Gold Wing's design, a luxury feature for a luxury motorcycle, and so looked at automotive cruise-control systems. One thing he was particularly interested in was how the cancelling procedures would differ between cars and motorcycles. The cruise control on a car normally cancels by operating the clutch or foot brake but, with the motorcycle system, the engineers added 'grip cancel' – turn the throttle and the system cancels. This became a standard for motorcycle cruise controls with other manufacturers following suit.

To make the LTD somewhat special Honda painted the bike Sunflash Gold Metallic with Valiant Brown Metallic panels, making it the first Gold Wing to be gold. They also increased the number of painted panels on the bike with the addition of one on each side of the faux tank and top-box lid. Beautiful Limited Edition eagle-like emblems on the fairing garnish and top-box hump, together with Limited Edition gold wording emblems on the sides of the panniers just set the bike off. The panniers had a new three-piece chrome and rubber bumper around them. The lower section was larger and reshaped to complement the longer, oval, turndown tailpipes of the exhaust. The top-box lid featured an aluminium handle for ease of opening along with an internal light, making it easier to see in the box at night. The signature light-bar had 'Gold Wing' across it. Colour-matched plastics became a feature of the LTD with the fairing internals and handlebar covers becoming Romany Red instead of black. The handlebars themselves were two part aluminium with a newly designed clamp cover that had small lights fitted to illuminate the stereo and 'Gold Wing' moulded in it. More ventilation was added to the lower fairing and the fairing lowers were redesigned to incorporate cornering lights; when indicating, the relevant light would illuminate, making corners easier to negotiate. The fairing and panniers featured additional side-marker lights, while the fairing mirror backs had an aluminium effect accent. The radiator featured a steel chrome trim with the Gold Wing logo stamped on the top section.

Each Limited Edition GL1200 was sold with a comprehensive tool kit, leather-bound owner's manual and a certificate of ownership. The certificate told the proud owner they were one of 5,372 to have bought this special motorcycle. The recommended retail price of the LTD was a staggering $10,000, the first five-figure Gold Wing, but Honda sold every single one in a short space of time. The Limited Edition was marketed officially in just two countries – the USA and Canada, the map feature on the ETC not being much use anywhere else!

Two new colours for the Interstate were offered, with Starshine Silver Metallic and Telstar Blue Metallic joining Candy Wineberry Red-U. The Aspencade was offered in three new colours – Satellite Blue Metallic, Pearl Vintage Red-A and Sandy Beige Metallic. For the 1985 model season, Honda (UK) imported just the Aspencade in the Sandy Beige Metallic, fortunately a lighter beige than the previous year, so it looked like a new model. At the time currency fluctuation was making it difficult for Honda to maintain their retail price and, in the UK, the Gold Wing increased in price by 11.22 per cent to £6,429.

Honda was expanding their operation in Ohio, USA and built the $30 million Anna Engine Plant (AEP), with production starting in July 1985. The first engines produced were for the 1986 GL1200s, which were then sent to Marysville for motorcycle production the following day.

The 1985 Limited Edition and 1986 Aspencade SE-i's Electronic Travel Computer. (Henning Kristiansen)

1986 GL1200IG Interstate, GL1200AG Aspencade and GL1200SE-iG Special Edition (Project ML8)

Relocating Gold Wing production to the USA was a smart move by Honda, as the tariffs President Reagan imposed earlier weren't really making any difference to them, but the next problem did – in just one year the US dollar fell more than 30 per cent against the Japanese yen on the currency markets, pushing prices up considerably. The problem wasn't isolated to the States; in Britain, Italian motorcycles became cheaper than Japanese ones for the first time.

It's always good to have some competition, but they were now producing even more bikes. Kawasaki added a smaller version of the Voyager to its range. The ZG1200 Voyager XII had an in-line four-cylinder, 1196cc engine, and the design of its luggage was very similar in shape to the GL1200. Yamaha updated their Venture Royale, increasing the engine size to 1300cc and totally redesigned the luggage, making it much larger, but only offering one model. Suzuki added a model to their line-up, offering three versions of the Cavalcade, with the new top-of-the-line LXE. This had the most gimmicky item ever fitted to a touring motorcycle, a passenger adjustable head-rest that was so high it made the bike look a little ridiculous.

Changes to the 1986 Gold Wing were slight, though some parts of the gear box were redesigned. The countershaft along with some gears featured smaller engagement slots for the gear dogs, which was done to improve driveline lash and make the transmission smoother and quieter. Redesigned hydraulic tappets had an increased oil capacity; this was to reduce valve-train noise. Valve timing was revised along with the redesigned exhaust downpipe; each was now a separate pipe, with the aim of getting more mid-range power with better power delivery. The Interstate had a new signature light-bar in the top-box fitted as standard. Previously the unit was a dummy, although the light-bar had been offered as an option. The once top-of-the-line Aspencade featured an updated instrument display with better illumination. The stereo now included Dolby and metal-tape capabilities.

Last year's Limited Edition owners weren't too happy with Honda. They thought they'd bought something special, but the bike was so successful Honda decided to release the LTD with different clothes in the form of the Aspencade SE-i (Special Edition-injected). Essentially the two bikes were the same, although Honda did make some improvements, painted it a different colour and lowered the price initially by $2. The Computerised-Fuel-Injection

Kawasaki's Voyager XII. Notice the luggage is very similar to the GL1200 Gold Wing. (Peter Rakestrow)

The author taking the 1986 GL1200 Aspencade SE-iG for a test ride. (Peter Rakestrow)

81

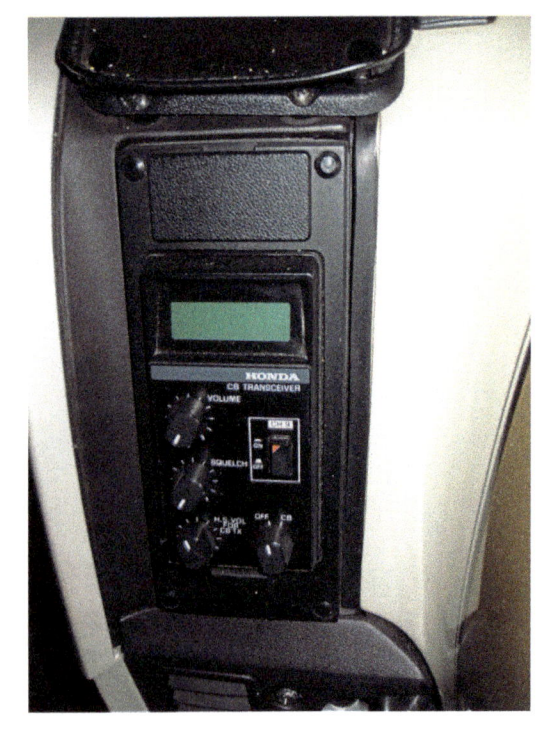

Above: The rear signature light of the GL1200 Aspencade SE-iG. (Henning Kristiansen)

Left: The GL1200 optional CB radio in the left lower fairing. (Henning Kristiansen)

system was revised to try and overcome the original problems and by reviewing the fuel pipes they managed to improve the vapor problem but, in reality, it created another problem, causing the bike to hesitate during cold morning startups. Some magazine tests of the LTD and SE-i weren't that impressed with the fuel injection system anyway, saying they thought the carburetted Aspencade gave better performance and fuel consumption. The Auto-Levelling-Rear-Suspension (ALRS) improved, with the predetermined rear-end setting getting stiffer, firming up the SE-i's ride. Special Edition emblems flanked the front fairing garnish and top-box lid, along with Aspencade and small SE-i emblems on the sides of each pannier. The tail-light signature told the driver behind that they were following an 'Aspencade SE-i'. The seat, internals of the fairing and handlebar covers were all still Romany Red in colour, while the bike's main colour was a new Pearl Splendor Ivory-A with Camel Beige Metallic panels and Maroon Metallic stripe. Honda only officially sold the SE-i in America. With the currency crisis the SE-i started with a price of $9,998, but soon headed up to $10,598.

In Britain things weren't looking too good as far as prices were concerned either. Honda imported more Deluxe models than Aspencades. The price for the Deluxe came in at £710 more than the previous 1984 model at £5,499, with a colour choice of Candy Wineberry Red-U. The Aspencade, on the other hand, only increasing £170 to £6,599 for the Pearl Marlin Blue-A colour. One other colour for the Interstate model was Black-Z, two other new Aspencade colours being Trophy Silver Metallic or Twilight Beige Metallic.

The redesigned paint graphics on the 1987 GL1200AH Aspencade. (Peter Rakestrow)

Engine covers on the 1987 GL1200AH Aspencade. The reason was to get owners used to more bodywork because of what was yet to come. (Peter Rakestrow)

The GL1200AH's fairing lower with optional cornering light, also note the belly-pan. (Peter Rakestrow)

Cruise control was now standard equipment on the American and Canadian 1987 GL1200 Aspencade models. (Peter Rakestrow)

1987 GL1200IH Interstate and GL1200AH Aspencade

This was to be the final year for the four-cylinder Gold Wing, although at the time we didn't know that the engine had run its course; it would have been difficult to increase its capacity in its current form as the casings were near their limit. Some GL1200s did suffer with blown head-gaskets due to its weak water jacket.

Honda offered only two models for 1987, the Interstate and the Aspencade, which returned to the top of the model line-up – gone was the expensive Aspencade SE-i. Honda extended the use of coloured plastics by making the Interstate's fairing internals Romany Red in colour. The Aspencade got the same treatment, but it did depend on the bike's main colour as to the colour of the internal fairing. The seat was all new, being deeper, much wider and made of triple-density foam. The last of any model should be the best and the 1987 Aspencade for the American and Canadian markets definitely was. They featured items from the LTD/SE-i, such as fairing lowers (without cornering lights, which were optional extras), extra ventilation, cruise control and the radiator chrome trim, as well as some additional items such as belly-pan and small engine side covers with aluminium effect trims. Three two-tone colours were offered: Black-Z, Candy Wineberry Red-U and new Pleiades Silver Metallic-U, which all had redesigned graphics. The two-tone panels on the top-box lid of the previous Aspencade model were discontinued and replaced by panels on the sides of the lid, which followed around the back of the bike. The panniers' panel complemented the lid's by being extended to nearly its full width so from the back they all matched, with the fairing side painted panels flowing in to the fairing side-trim.

An American-specification 1987 GL1200AH Aspencade with all the extra body work. (American Honda Motor Co. Inc.)

A very heavily chrome-accessorised 1984 GL1200AE Gold Wing Aspencade. Most parts are from the Drag Specialties catalogue. (Peter Rakestrow)

With the niche UK market for Gold Wings it was amazing Honda (UK) brought the 1987 model in at all. Unfortunately the bike was nothing like the US or Canadian models; the British market only had the Candy Wineberry Red-U colour with the new graphics and new seat, but none of the real goodies. There was an inexorable price rise in January to £7,999, up 19.4 per cent from the previous year's bike, and in April the price increased by another £400. The number of Aspencades Honda (UK) imported was just thirty, making it a very rare machine indeed but, with all those price hikes, I'm not surprised.

The Gold Wing has continued to evolve throughout the years. One interesting thing about this first part of its history is that, although the Gold Wing was produced in Japan initially, none of the four-cylinder Gold Wings were officially sold there. It wasn't until March 1988 that Honda sold its first Gold Wing, a GL1500, to the Japanese public. But that's another story!

Specifications

GL1200 1984–1987

Dimensions
Overall length	STD	2,355 mm (92.7 inches)
	INT/Deluxe/ASP/LTD/SE-i	2,505 mm (98.6 inches)
Overall width		970 mm (38.2 inches)
Overall height	STD	1,170 mm (46.1 inches)
	INT/Deluxe/ASP/LTD/SE-i	1,510 mm (59.4 inches)
Wheel base		1,610 mm (63.4 inches)
Ground clearance		140 mm (5.5 inches)

Weight
Dry weight

	STD	272 kg (600 lbs)
	INT/Deluxe	317 kg (699 lbs)
	ASP	328 kg (723 lbs) [328 kg (723 lbs)]
	ASP ('85/'86)	330 kg (728 lbs) [329 kg (725 lbs)]
	ASP ('87)	337 kg (743 lbs) [329 kg (725 lbs)]
	LTD/SE-i	355 kg (782 lbs)

Engine
Bore and stroke   75.5 × 66 mm (2.97 × 2.59 inches)
Compression ratio   9.0:1
Displacement   1,181cc (72.1 cu-in)
Carburettors   4 × 32 mm CV Type
Power output   94 bhp @ 7,000 rpm

Power transmission		1984	1985/'86	1987
Primary reduction		1.708	1.708	1.708
Secondary reduction		0.897	0.973	0.976
Gear Ratio	1st.	2.643	2.571	2.571
	2nd.	1.667	1.667	1.667
	3rd.	1.250	1.250	1.250
	4th.	1.000	1.000	1.000
	5th.	0.829	0.800	0.800
Final reduction		2.830	2.833	2.833

Chassis and suspension
Castor   60 degree
Trail   118 mm (4.6 inches)
Tyre size   Front   130/90-16 67H Tubeless
                Rear   150/90-15 74H Tubeless

Electrical
Battery   12v – 20AH
Generator output   360 watt @ 5,000 rpm A.C. Three phase
                  LTD/.SE-i   490 watt @ 5,000 rpm A.C. Three phase

Notes: [ ] UK type

5

The UK Special, the Executive

This bike was the brainchild of Gerald Davidson who at the time was head of the motorcycle division at Honda (UK) in Chiswick. The Executives were produced as a marketing exercise. Gerald Davidson saw it as an opportunity to give Honda's flagship the status it deserved, so Honda commissioned Rickman, of New Milton, Hampshire, to design the bike. Rickman already had a good relationship with Honda as they manufactured all the Honda-style fairings, engine bars, racks and luggage.

The bike started life as a GL1000K1 and first appeared in *Motorcycle News*'s Mark-the-Ball competition on 5 January 1977 with the prize valued at £2,200. The bike built for *MCN.* was designated an 'Executive Gold Wing' on the side panels, was painted black with gold air-brushing, and had a Rickman type 5 fairing, Rickman crash bars and rear carrier. It also had Lester cast alloy wheels that were 16-inch rear (as opposed to the 17-inch standard wire wheel) and 19-inch front, fitted with Avon Roadrunner tyres. The person who won the bike was thirty-eight-year-old Tony Minchin from Yate, near Bristol. He worked as a HGV fitter, had owned twenty bikes over the years and had two attempts at the competition. His stake was a massive 75 pence.

Rickman's then advertising manager, Bill Hawker, designed the paint scheme and 'Executive' decals. When asked by the author, Bill explained that although 'the project was quite straight forward, one problem we did have initially was getting the paint to stick to the plastic side panels.'

The paint work and air-brushing was done by a custom paint sprayer called Clive Miles, who was located in Verwood, not a million miles from Rickman's factory. The first challenge Clive had was to remove the original Gold Wing decals and pinstriping from the plastic side panels, which were underneath a clear top coat. Once the panel had been flatted down, a primer coat was then added, but every primer Clive used reacted with the original paint, so he went back to his paint supplier to see what they could do. After sending the painted parts to a laboratory for investigation a special primer was made to overcome the problem. Clive then sprayed all the parts black and air-brushed the gold pinstriping.

The seats were sent to a company called P & P Seating in Birmingham – the owners of the company, Oliver and John Plunket, were also the designers. The material chosen was

Above: Gold Wing Executive number 23, in original condition with after-market top-box. (Peter Rakestrow)

Right: The GL1000K1 Executive certificate signed by Gerald Davidson on behalf of Honda UK. (Brian Hemmings)

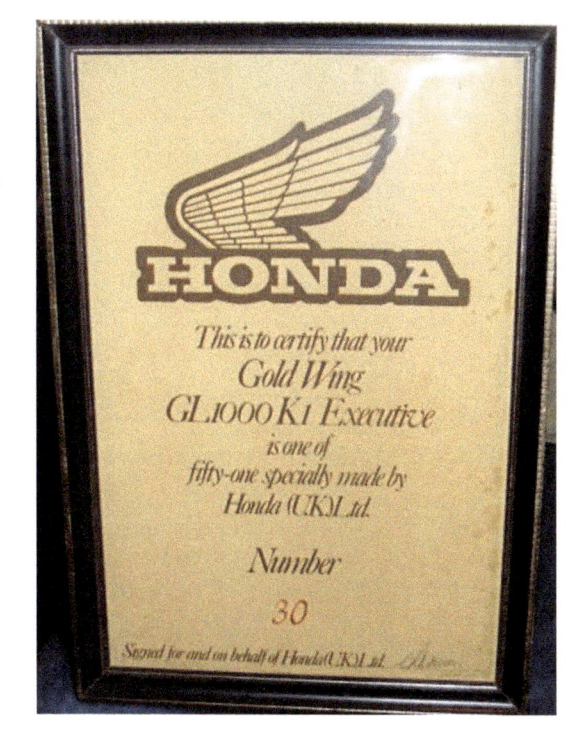

a brown leather-looking vinyl called naugahide, normally used for making throw-over saddlebags. The seats had to be designed to the limitation of the material, because it was a lot thicker than normal vinyl, so they were made in six sections before being stitched together. One thing Oliver and John did was make sure the rider and passenger weren't seated directly on the stitched areas as they were double the thickness and would have been very uncomfortable, though the GL1000 seat was not renowned for its comfort anyway. 'Honda Gold Wing Executive' was then hot-foil printed on the back in gold.

The wheels were purchased from David Smith at Lester Wheels UK, the distributor of the American-made wheels. One other small problem Bill Hawker faced was disposing of the fifty-two sets of brand-new wire wheels!

In the spring of 1977, issue No.1 of *Hondaway*, the official magazine for Honda owners, ran an article on the Gold Wing Executive. The front cover pictured Dinah May, one of Honda's models, dressed in green and yellow Honda leathers and sitting astride Gold Wing Executive number 001. 'A numbered series of only 100 machines are to be built to specific orders only', they said. The article continued to say the bikes would be similar to the one built for *MCN*. 'In addition to each machine bearing its series number 001–100 the owner will receive a certificate of ownership. Late February/early March'. According to Honda's advert the price was to be £2,300 plus 8 per cent VAT.

The numbered bikes differed only slightly from the original done for *MCN*'s Mark-the-Ball competition. The side cover decals had been changed – instead of 'Executive Gold Wing' they were 'Gold Wing Executive' and had a circled place for the serial number. A VDO clock

The rear of the naugahide-covered Executive's seat. (Peter Rakestrow)

was added, mounted on the information light console between the speedo and tachometer. The windscreen had a blue tint. The seats were brown as opposed to the original black of the *MCN* bike. Number 001, which Honda used in their promotional literature, had its decals hand painted in gold leaf. The framed certificate stated that the 'Gold Wing GL1000 K1 Executive was one of fifty-one'. In total, fifty-two Executives were built by Rickman Brothers and very few remain in original condition, with some being sold by owners and exported to Europe and America.

6

Moving to America

Plans for an American manufacturing operation started in 1974 with a feasibility study for a car plant but, because of the friction between the Japanese and American auto trades, it was decided to build a motorcycle plant instead. The study found that Ohio offered good transportation, geographical proximity to component suppliers and the abundance of high-quality labour.

On 11 October 1977 Honda announced that they would build a $35 million facility near Marysville, Ohio, which would be called Marysville Motorcycle Plant (MMP) and be designed purely to build the Gold Wing. When visiting the site Soichiro Honda was asked at a press interview, 'why Ohio?' He answered, 'It was a divine revelation'. Honda America Manufacturing's (HAM) President, Kazuo Nakagawa, along with Ohio State Governor James Rhodes, broke ground for the new factory on 3 April 1978 and just seventeen months later MMP produced its first motorcycle. Honda recruited labour locally, generally farm workers with no experience of building a motorcycle. On 10 September 1979, the first task for the original sixty-four associates (Honda's term for its employees) was to build the CR250R Elsinore, a red dirt bike – just ten machines were completed on that day. The CR250R was deemed by Honda management as a simple machine to build before their associates were trusted to build a much more complex machine such as the Gold Wing.

Just two months later Honda associates started production of the air-cooled six-cylinder CBX1000. It wasn't until May 1980 that they started production of the GL1100 Gold Wing and by the year's end HAM associates had produced nearly 16,000 of them – associate numbers had also increased from sixty-four to 356. By 23 April 1982 the Marysville plant had produced its 100,000th machine, which was a 1982 Sterling Silver Metallic-U GL1100 Gold Wing Aspencade. This was the first milestone broken by the associates and Honda announced an expansion program to upgrade the paint shop. MMP wasn't just a 260,000 sq. ft assembly facility, it also produced frames, saddlebags and top-boxes, fairings and mudguards. Plastic components were injection moulded and painted in house. Engines and drivetrains still came from Japan. Ed Buker, the MMP manufacturing manager in the mid-eighties, told *Wing Elite* magazine that the motorcycle plant kept 'less than two day's inventory on hand' and that 'about 50 per cent of material used in a new Gold Wing is local content'.

Honda of America Manufacturing president Kazuo Nakagawa rides the first HAM-built motorcycle off the production line, a CR250R Elsinore, on 10 September 1979. (American Honda Motor Co. Inc.)

On 1 June 1983 production started on the all-new Gold Wing, the GL1200, which was the first complete model change with which the HAM associates had been involved. Later that month Soichiro Honda made a return visit to the plant to see for himself the great achievement of his American associates, as generally the American car and motorcycle industries didn't have a good reputation for build quality.

Rapid growth of Honda's manufacturing facilities in Ohio continued. HAM announced on 8 March 1984 that they would invest $30 million to build an engine plant in nearby Anna, which was to produce engines for the Gold Wing and later the VT1100C Shadow. On 22 July 1985 production started at the Anna Engine Plant (AEP) on the GL1200 engine, with ninety-one associates producing twenty engines a day – each complete engine was built by a single associate. The first engine was installed into a 1986 Interstate, which was the beginning of the 'All American Gold Wing' 'Made In The USA', of which associates in Anna and Marysville were very proud. It took just six months for the AEP associates to achieve their first milestone by completing 10,000 engines, all of which were Gold Wings.

Although the intention was to build the engine for the VT1100C Shadow at AEP, a decision early in 1986 was made to build the Civic car engine instead and production of the 1.5-litre four-cylinder Civic engine started on 23 September 1986. At the time the Anna Engine Plant was the only factory in the world to build both motorcycle and car engines under one roof, with Gold Wing engines being built on the first shift, early in the morning on 'Zero Line'. All motorcycle engine production would be sent to the Marysville motorcycle plant, ready for motorcycle assembly the following day.

At its peak the Marysville Motorcycle Plant could produce 150 motorcycles a day with average Gold Wing production of seventy-four; normally build patterns were in batches of ten, so as to break any monotony for the associates. From its inception to the end of the 1987 model year MMP built eleven other motorcycles including CB900 Custom, VF1100 Sabre and the CBR1000 Hurricane.

1986 all-American Gold Wings. An Aspencade and Aspencade SE-i in front of the Marysville factory, along with some memorabilia. (Peter Rakestrow.)

Acknowledgements

Honda Motor Co. Ltd Japan.
American Honda Motor Co., Inc.
Bonhams of London.
Barry W. Benkert, Sr, for allowing me to use his photo of Harry Ward.
Deutsches Zweirad- und NSU-Museum in Neckarsulm, Germany – well worth a visit.
Tim Brooks, Chairman of GWOCGB for passing this opportunity on to me.
Henning Kristiansen, for the use of some of his photographs.
Brian Hemmings, for the use of his photograph.
Rob Anstey, for helping me with the cover photograph.
Mark Rakestrow, for helping me design and build my cut-away GL1000 engine.
Jim Razey.
Jim Hill.
Ray Brooking.
John Williams.
Janine Dickens.
Wendy Rakestrow, for being so understanding and for her help with this book.